THE DR. NOW 1200-CALORIE DIET PLAN

Reclaim your life and health with Dr. Now's 1200-calorie diet solution°simple recipes, proven methods, and a plan to regain energy and confidence in just 30 days.

Ethan Wellborne

© **Copyright 2024 by** Ethan Wellborne **- All rights reserved.**

The following book is provided below with the aim of delivering information that is as precise and dependable as possible. However, purchasing this book implies an acknowledgment that both the publisher and the author are not experts in the discussed topics, and any recommendations or suggestions contained herein are solely for entertainment purposes. It is advised that professionals be consulted as needed before acting on any endorsed actions.

This statement is considered fair and valid by both the American Bar Association and the Committee of Publishers Association, and it holds legal binding throughout the United States.

Moreover, any transmission, duplication, or reproduction of this work, including specific information, will be deemed an illegal act, regardless of whether it is done electronically or in print. This includes creating secondary or tertiary copies of the work or recorded copies, which are only allowed with the express written consent from the Publisher. All additional rights are reserved.

The information in the following pages is generally considered to be a truthful and accurate account of facts. As such, any negligence, use, or misuse of the information by the reader will result in actions falling solely under their responsibility. There are no scenarios in which the publisher or the original author can be held liable for any difficulties or damages that may occur after undertaking the information described herein.

Additionally, the information in the following pages is intended solely for informational purposes and should be considered as such. As fitting its nature, it is presented without assurance regarding its prolonged validity or interim quality. Mention of trademarks is done without written consent and should not be construed as an endorsement from the trademark holder.

TABLE OF CONTENTS

INTRODUCTION ... 11
- Welcome to Your Journey ... 11
- The Purpose of This Book ... 11
- Why Dr. Now's 1200-Calorie Diet Works ... 11
- Understanding the Challenges ... 12
- Common Struggles in Weight Loss ... 12
- How This Plan Addresses Your Needs ... 12
- A Note from Dr. Nowzaradan ... 13
- Inspiration and Motivation to Begin ... 13

CHAPTER 1: THE SCIENCE BEHIND THE PLAN ... 14
- Dr. Nowzaradan's Philosophy ... 14
- High-Protein, Low-Carb, Low-Fat Principles ... 14
- The Role of Hydration and Portion Control ... 15
- The Impact of Obesity ... 16
- Physical and Emotional Health Challenges ... 16
- Scientific Benefits of Losing Weight ... 17
- How 1200 Calories Make a Difference ... 17
- Understanding Caloric Deficits ... 18
- Why This Calorie Count is Effective for Rapid, Safe Weight Loss ... 18

CHAPTER 2: GETTING STARTED ... 20
- Setting Realistic Goals ... 20
- How to Measure Success Beyond the Scale ... 20
- Understanding Your Caloric Needs ... 21
- Adapting the 1200-Calorie Plan to Your Body ... 21
- Tools for Success ... 22
- What You'll Need: Scales, Meal Prep Containers, and More ... 22
- How to Use This Book Effectively ... 23

CHAPTER 3: MEAL PLANNING MADE SIMPLE 24

Structuring Your Day 24
How to Balance Meals for Energy and Satisfaction 24
Meal Frequency: 3 Main Meals + 1 Snack 25
Shopping Made Easy 25
Budget-Friendly Grocery Lists 26
Essential Pantry Staples 26
Weekly Meal Plans 27
Sample Menus for Week 1 and Beyond 27

CHAPTER 4: RECIPES FOR EVERY OCCASION 29

BREAKFASTS 29

- Quinoa and Chia Seed Porridge 29
- Avocado and Smoked Salmon Toast 30
- Sweet Potato and Black Bean Breakfast Hash 31
- Spinach and Feta Omelette 32
- Overnight Oats with Apple and Cinnamon 33
- Zucchini and Tomato Frittata 33
- Banana and Almond Butter Smoothie 34
- Whole Wheat Pancakes with Berries 35

Energizing Options to Start Your Day 36

LUNCHES 37

- Quinoa-Stuffed Bell Peppers 37
- Spicy Lentil and Sweet Potato Stew 38
- Chickpea and Avocado Salad Wrap 39
- Grilled Eggplant and Tomato Stack 40
- Curried Cauliflower Rice Bowl 41
- Spinach and Feta Stuffed Portobello Mushrooms 41
- Roasted Beet and Orange Salad 42
- Zucchini Noodles with Pesto and Cherry Tomatoes 43

Portable and Satisfying Meals for Work or Home 44

DINNERS 45

Spiced Lentil and Pumpkin Stew 45

Herb-Crusted Cod with Lemon Aioli 46

Quinoa-Stuffed Bell Peppers 47

Chickpea and Spinach Curry 48

Turmeric Cauliflower Steaks 49

Sesame Ginger Tofu Stir-Fry 49

Miso Glazed Eggplant 50

Zucchini Noodles with Avocado Pesto 51

FAMILY-FRIENDLY RECIPES UNDER 300 CALORIES 52

Spiced Chickpea and Kale Sauté 52

Herbed Quinoa and Edamame Salad 53

Sweet Potato and Black Bean Tacos 54

Curried Cauliflower Soup 55

Ginger-Lime Grilled Shrimp 56

Zesty Lemon Herb Chicken 57

Roasted Beet and Feta Salad 58

Eggplant and Lentil Stew 59

SNACKS AND DESSERTS 59

Chia and Matcha Energy Bites 59

Spicy Avocado Hummus 60

Quinoa and Pomegranate Parfait 61

Roasted Chickpeas with Smoked Paprika 62

Frozen Yogurt Bark with Berries 63

Sweet Potato and Black Bean Mini Tacos 63

Coconut and Lime Chia Pudding 64

Spiced Apple and Walnut Muffins 65

GUILT-FREE INDULGENCES TO STAY ON TRACK 66

- Spiced Chickpea and Quinoa Salad 66
- Herbed Cauliflower Rice with Almonds 67
- Roasted Red Pepper Hummus 68
- Eggplant Caponata 69
- Zucchini Noodles with Avocado Pesto 70
- Sweet Potato and Black Bean Tacos 71
- Baked Falafel with Tahini Sauce 72
- Pumpkin and Lentil Curry 73

CHAPTER 5: PRACTICAL TIPS FOR SUCCESS 74

- Portion Control and Serving Sizes 75
- How to Measure Portions Without Stress 75
- Managing Cr Indulgences to Stay on Trackavings and Emotional Eating 76
- Strategies to Stay in Control 76
- Staying Motivated 77
- Overcoming Setbacks and Plateaus 77
- Dining Out and Social Situations 77
- How to Navigate Menus and Stay Compliant 78

CHAPTER 6: ADAPTING THE PLAN FOR YOUR NEEDS 78

- Special Dietary Considerations 79
- Adjusting for Allergies, Vegetarian Options, and More 79
- Cultural and Personal Preferences 80
- Substitutions for Common Ingredients 80

CHAPTER 7: MOVING BEYOND THE PLATE 81

- The Role of Exercise 82
- Why Physical Activity Enhances Weight Loss 82
- Beginner-Friendly Exercises for Limited Mobility 83
- Mindset and Mental Health 83
- Building Confidence and Overcoming Self-Doubt 84

CHAPTER 8: SAMPLE 30-DAY MEAL PLAN 84
Week-by-Week Breakdown 85

COMPLETE MENUS WITH RECIPES AND PREP TIPS 85
- Spiced Quinoa and Chickpea Bowl 85
- Herbed Zucchini Noodles with Walnut Pesto 86
- Turmeric-Infused Cauliflower Steaks 87
- Avocado and Black Bean Stuffed Peppers 88
- Ginger-Sesame Soba Noodles 89
- Lemon-Dill Baked Cod 90
- Roasted Beet and Orange Salad 91
- Spicy Lentil and Tomato Stew 91

Tracking Your Progress 92
How to Use the Included Journal Effectively 93

CHAPTER 9: FINAL WORDS OF ENCOURAGEMENT 93
What to Expect After 30 Days 94
Sustaining Your Weight Loss 94
Transitioning to Long-Term Healthy Habits 95
Your Journey to a Healthier, Happier Life 95
Staying Committed to Your Goals 96

APPENDICES 96
Understanding Nutritional Labels 96
Meal Planning Tips 97
Staying Motivated 97
Food Lists: Recommended and Avoided Items 97
Substitution Guide: Budget and Taste-Friendly Options 98

FAQS: COMMON QUESTIONS ANSWERED 98
How can I ensure I'm getting enough nutrients? 98

What if I feel hungry all the time? 98
Can I still enjoy social gatherings? 98
How do I handle setbacks? 99
Is exercise necessary on this plan? 99

INTRODUCTION

Welcome to a journey of transformation, where each step is a stride toward a healthier, more vibrant you. In the pages ahead, you'll discover the power of the **Dr. Now 1200-Calorie Diet Plan**, a method designed not just to shed pounds, but to reclaim your life. This isn't merely a diet; it's a gateway to renewed **energy and confidence**, crafted with care and backed by science.

Imagine waking up each day feeling lighter, not just in weight but in spirit. Picture yourself navigating the world with newfound **vitality**, unburdened by the physical and emotional weight that once held you back. This is **more** than possible—it's within reach.

Throughout this book, you'll find a blend of **practical advice** and heartfelt motivation. My goal is to be your guide, offering insights that are as empathetic as they are informative. Together, we'll tackle challenges and celebrate victories, ensuring that your path to wellness is not only effective but also **sustainable**.

WELCOME TO YOUR JOURNEY

Embarking on this journey is about more than just shedding pounds; it's about reclaiming your life. Imagine waking up each day with **renewed energy** and a sense of purpose. This isn't a quick fix or a temporary solution; it's a commitment to a healthier, more fulfilling lifestyle.

As you begin, remind yourself that every step forward is a triumph. You might face challenges, and that's okay. Remember, it's not about perfection; it's about **progress**. Celebrate each small victory, whether it's choosing a healthier meal or taking a brisk walk. These moments accumulate, leading to significant change.

Surround yourself with a **supportive community**, be it family, friends, or others on a similar path. Their encouragement can be a powerful motivator. Allow yourself to feel proud of your efforts, and know that you're not alone. Together, we're building a foundation for a healthier, happier future.

THE PURPOSE OF THIS BOOK

Embarking on a journey to better health can be daunting, yet it's also a profound opportunity to reclaim your life. This book is crafted as a **companion and guide**, designed to lead you through the intricacies of the **1200-calorie diet** with empathy and precision. Here, you will find not just a plan, but a pathway to **sustainable change** that respects your unique circumstances and challenges.

Our shared goal is to help you achieve **safe and effective weight loss**, improved well-being, and a harmonious balance between personal health goals and social dynamics. This isn't merely about shedding pounds; it's about gaining **confidence, energy, and a renewed sense of self**. Together, we'll navigate the emotional hurdles, address the logistical challenges, and celebrate the victories, big and small.

Remember, this is a journey of empowerment, where each step forward is a testament to your strength and determination. Let's begin this transformative adventure together, with optimism and unwavering support.

WHY DR. NOW'S 1200-CALORIE DIET WORKS

Dr. Now's 1200-calorie diet is not just another fad; it's a scientifically backed approach that has helped countless individuals reclaim their health. The magic lies in its simplicity and effectiveness. By consuming just 1200 calories a day, you create a **caloric deficit**, which is essential for weight loss. But what sets this plan apart is its focus on **nutrient-dense foods**. You're not just cutting calories; you're fueling your body with the right nutrients that promote **energy** and **well-being**.

Many struggle with the emotional aspects of dieting, but this plan addresses those challenges head-on. It's designed to be **flexible** and **adaptable**, allowing you to incorporate your favorite foods while staying within your calorie limit. This flexibility helps reduce feelings of deprivation and makes it easier to stick to the plan long-term.

Moreover, the diet encourages **mindful eating**. By paying attention to your hunger cues and savoring each bite, you learn to appreciate food more and make healthier choices naturally. This approach not only aids in weight loss but also fosters a healthier relationship with food, setting you up for **sustainable success**.

UNDERSTANDING THE CHALLENGES

Embarking on a weight loss journey can feel overwhelming, especially when faced with the challenge of adhering to a **1200-calorie diet**. It's not just about reducing calories; it's about understanding and navigating the **emotional and psychological hurdles** that accompany such a significant lifestyle change. Many find themselves grappling with **emotional eating**, where food becomes a source of comfort rather than nourishment. This can create a cycle of frustration and guilt, making it difficult to stay on track.

Moreover, the **social dynamics** of dieting can be daunting. Whether it's attending family gatherings or dining out with friends, the pressure to conform to social norms can lead to feelings of isolation or discouragement. It's crucial to remember that these challenges are not insurmountable. By focusing on your **goals** and the positive changes you're making, you can transform these obstacles into stepping stones toward a healthier, more fulfilling life.

COMMON STRUGGLES IN WEIGHT LOSS

Embarking on a weight loss journey is often a path filled with **unexpected challenges**. One of the most common hurdles is the emotional struggle. Many find themselves battling **emotional eating**, where stress or comfort leads to consuming foods that derail progress. Recognizing these triggers is the first step toward overcoming them.

Another challenge is managing the **logistical aspects** of a 1200-calorie diet. Planning meals within this limit can feel overwhelming, especially when juggling family and social obligations. It's essential to find a balance that allows for flexibility without compromising your goals.

Budget constraints also play a significant role. The perception that healthy eating is expensive can be discouraging. However, with strategic planning, it's possible to source affordable, diet-compliant foods that nourish both body and wallet.

Lastly, facing **social and familial pressure** can be daunting. It's crucial to cultivate a support system that understands and respects your commitment to change, ensuring your journey is both sustainable and fulfilling.

HOW THIS PLAN ADDRESSES YOUR NEEDS

Embarking on a journey toward better health can feel overwhelming, especially when faced with the challenge of following a **1200-calorie diet**. This plan is designed to meet your needs by providing a **sustainable approach** that fits seamlessly into your life. By focusing on **simple, nutritious meals**, you'll find it easier to stick to your goals without sacrificing flavor or satisfaction.

We understand that **emotional eating** can be a hurdle. Our plan offers strategies to help you recognize and manage these triggers, empowering you to make healthier choices. Additionally, the plan considers **budget constraints**, offering affordable options that won't break the bank.

Social and familial support is crucial. By including meals that cater to **family dynamics**, this plan fosters an environment where everyone can thrive together. Remember, change is a journey, not a destination. With each step, you're reclaiming your **energy and confidence**, paving the way for a healthier, more fulfilling life.

A Note from Dr. Nowzaradan

Embarking on a journey towards better health can feel daunting, but it's a path worth taking. With the **Dr. Now 1200-Calorie Diet Plan**, you're not just starting a diet; you're embracing a **lifestyle transformation**. Our bodies are remarkable machines, and by nourishing them properly, we unlock a world of energy and vitality.

Many of us struggle with emotional eating, often turning to food for comfort. This plan is designed to help you recognize and overcome these challenges, providing not only a dietary framework but also the **emotional support** needed to succeed. Remember, you are not alone in this journey. Each step you take is a step towards a healthier, more fulfilling life.

Let this guide be your companion, offering **empathetic guidance** and practical strategies. Together, we will navigate the complexities of weight loss, building a foundation for lasting change. Your health and happiness are within reach.

Inspiration and Motivation to Begin

Starting your journey toward a healthier lifestyle can feel daunting, but it's important to remember that **every small step counts**. Embrace the idea of progress over perfection. It's not about making drastic changes overnight, but about taking consistent, manageable steps toward your goals.

Visualize the **benefits of your transformation**—more energy, improved self-esteem, and a greater sense of well-being. Imagine the joy of engaging in activities you love without feeling held back. This vision can be a powerful motivator on tough days.

Remember, you're not alone. Many have walked this path and found success through determination and support. Surround yourself with a **community that understands** your journey, whether it's friends, family, or online groups. Share your challenges and triumphs; you'll find strength in connection.

Finally, celebrate every victory, no matter how small. Each step forward is a testament to your commitment and courage. Keep moving forward, and soon, you'll find yourself living the healthier, more vibrant life you deserve.

CHAPTER 1: THE SCIENCE BEHIND THE PLAN

Imagine standing at the crossroads of health, where the decision to embark on a transformative journey begins. This is where science meets aspiration, guiding you through the intricacies of weight loss. **Understanding the science** behind the 1200-calorie diet plan is akin to having a roadmap for success. It's not just about eating less; it's about **nourishing your body** in a way that promotes both weight loss and overall well-being.

The foundation of this plan lies in the concept of **caloric deficit**. Simply put, consuming fewer calories than your body burns leads to weight loss. However, it's crucial to ensure that these calories are packed with **essential nutrients** to maintain health and vitality. Think of your body as a finely tuned machine; it requires the right fuel to function optimally.

Consider the role of **macronutrients**—proteins, fats, and carbohydrates. Each plays a pivotal role in your diet. Proteins not only help in muscle repair but also keep you feeling full, reducing the urge to snack unnecessarily. Healthy fats are vital for brain function and hormone production, while carbohydrates provide the energy needed for daily activities. Balancing these macronutrients is key to a successful diet.

As you delve into this plan, remember that it's not just about numbers on a scale. It's about reclaiming your life, your health, and your confidence. Embrace the journey with an open mind and a determined heart, knowing that each step brings you closer to a healthier, more vibrant you.

Dr. Nowzaradan's Philosophy

Dr. Nowzaradan's philosophy is rooted in a profound understanding of the **human struggle** with weight loss. His approach is not just about shedding pounds; it's about transforming lives. At the core of his method is the belief that **change begins in the mind**. He advocates for a mental shift where individuals see themselves not as victims of their circumstances but as **active participants** in their health journey.

Central to his philosophy is the idea that **simplicity and consistency** are key. The 1200-calorie diet is a tool, not a punishment. It's designed to be **manageable and sustainable**, allowing people to focus on what truly matters: regaining control over their lives. Dr. Now emphasizes that each meal is an opportunity to make a choice that aligns with one's goals, fostering a sense of **empowerment and autonomy**.

Dr. Nowzaradan also understands the **emotional complexities** tied to eating. He encourages addressing underlying emotional triggers, promoting a holistic view of health that includes both physical and mental well-being. His empathetic approach reassures individuals that setbacks are part of the process, and what matters most is the **commitment to keep moving forward**.

High-Protein, Low-Carb, Low-Fat Principles

As you embark on this transformative journey, understanding the core principles of a high-protein, low-carb, low-fat diet will be your guiding light. This approach is not just about shedding pounds; it's about embracing a lifestyle that fuels your body with the **right nutrients** while keeping your energy levels steady and your cravings in check.

First, let's delve into the importance of **protein**. Often hailed as the building block of life, protein plays a pivotal role in maintaining muscle mass, especially as you lose weight. By incorporating lean sources such as chicken, fish, tofu, and legumes, you ensure that your body receives the essential amino acids it needs to repair and build tissues. This not only aids in weight loss but also supports a healthy metabolism.

Next, we address the role of **carbohydrates**. While carbs have gotten a bad rap in many diet circles, it's crucial to understand that not all carbs are created equal. The key is to focus on **complex carbohydrates**, which are digested slowly, providing a steady release of energy. Think whole grains, vegetables, and fruits. These foods are rich in fiber, helping you feel full longer and reducing the temptation to snack on less healthy options.

Now, let's talk about **fats**. Contrary to popular belief, fat is not the enemy. However, the type of fat you consume makes all the difference. Prioritize healthy fats found in foods like avocados, nuts, and olive oil. These fats support brain health and can help reduce inflammation, making them an essential part of your diet.

Balancing these macronutrients is about more than just numbers; it's about listening to your body and understanding its needs. As you adjust to this dietary framework, you might notice increased energy, improved mood, and even better sleep. These are signs that your body is responding positively to the changes you're making.

Remember, the journey to a healthier you is not a sprint; it's a marathon. There will be days when sticking to the plan feels challenging, and that's okay. The important thing is to stay committed and recognize that each choice you make is a step towards reclaiming your health and vitality.

As you continue, keep in mind that this is not just a diet—it's a lifestyle change. Embrace the process, celebrate your victories, and learn from any setbacks. With patience and persistence, the high-protein, low-carb, low-fat principles will become second nature, guiding you to a healthier, more fulfilling life.

THE ROLE OF HYDRATION AND PORTION CONTROL

When embarking on a journey to better health, two often overlooked yet **vital components** are hydration and portion control. These elements, while seemingly simple, can profoundly influence your success on the 1200-calorie diet plan.

Firstly, let's talk about **hydration**. Water is not just a thirst quencher; it's a fundamental part of our body's daily operations. Staying hydrated helps to regulate body temperature, keeps joints lubricated, and aids in digestion. More importantly, it can play a crucial role in weight loss. Often, our bodies confuse thirst with hunger, leading us to consume extra calories when a glass of water would suffice. By drinking water regularly throughout the day, you can help curb unnecessary snacking and maintain your focus on your dietary goals.

Incorporating water-rich foods like cucumbers, watermelon, and strawberries into your diet can also enhance your hydration levels while providing essential nutrients. Remember, starting your day with a glass of water can set a positive tone, giving your metabolism a gentle nudge to kickstart the day.

Now, let's delve into **portion control**. In a world where oversized meals have become the norm, understanding the right portion sizes is crucial. Portion control is not about deprivation; it's about **mindful eating**. By being conscious of the amount of food you consume, you can enjoy a variety of foods without exceeding your calorie limits.

One practical method is using smaller plates and bowls. This simple trick can help you perceive your meals as more substantial, reducing the temptation to overeat. Additionally, paying attention to your body's hunger cues and eating slowly can prevent overeating. Allow yourself to savor each bite, and stop when you feel satisfied, not stuffed.

Incorporating these strategies into your daily routine requires patience and practice. But with time, they will become second nature, supporting your journey towards a healthier, more energetic you. Remember, every sip and every bite is a step towards reclaiming your health and confidence.

THE IMPACT OF OBESITY

Obesity is more than just a number on the scale; it's a complex health issue that affects every aspect of life. From physical health to emotional well-being, the impact of carrying excess weight can be profound. Many individuals experience a range of **health complications** linked to obesity, including diabetes, heart disease, and joint problems. These conditions not only affect longevity but also significantly reduce quality of life, making everyday activities more challenging.

Beyond the physical, the emotional toll of obesity can be equally overwhelming. Many people struggle with feelings of **self-doubt** and **low self-esteem**, often exacerbated by societal pressures and stigmatization. This emotional burden can lead to a cycle of stress and emotional eating, further complicating weight management efforts.

Moreover, obesity can strain **social relationships** and family dynamics. Navigating social settings where food is central, like family gatherings or dining out with friends, can be daunting. The fear of judgment or misunderstanding from loved ones can create a sense of isolation, making it harder to stay committed to a healthy lifestyle.

Financial constraints also play a role. Accessing healthy, affordable food options can be a significant barrier for many. The perception that healthy eating is costly adds another layer of difficulty, making it seem impossible to adhere to a structured diet plan.

Understanding these challenges is crucial for creating a supportive environment where individuals feel empowered to make lasting changes. By recognizing the multifaceted impact of obesity, we can develop strategies that address both the physical and emotional aspects of weight loss, paving the way for a healthier, more fulfilling life.

PHYSICAL AND EMOTIONAL HEALTH CHALLENGES

When embarking on a weight loss journey, the intertwining of **physical** and **emotional health** challenges can feel overwhelming. This chapter aims to address these hurdles, offering guidance and support as you strive for a healthier lifestyle.

First, let's recognize the **physical challenges** that often accompany weight loss. You may experience fatigue or reduced energy levels as your body adjusts to a lower calorie intake. It's crucial to listen to your body and ensure you're getting adequate rest. Incorporating light physical activity, such as walking or stretching, can help boost your energy without overexerting yourself.

On the **emotional front**, the journey can be equally demanding. Weight loss often brings to light deep-seated emotions tied to body image and self-worth. It's important to acknowledge these feelings rather than suppress them. Consider journaling or speaking with a supportive friend or therapist to process your emotions constructively.

Another common emotional hurdle is dealing with **emotional eating**. Food often serves as a comfort during stressful times, and breaking this cycle requires patience and mindfulness. Start by identifying triggers and replacing them with healthier coping mechanisms, like meditation or engaging in a hobby.

Lastly, navigating **social dynamics** can be challenging. Friends or family may unintentionally undermine your efforts with comments or behaviors. Open communication is key. Share your goals with loved ones and seek their support, explaining how they can help you stay on track.

Remember, you're not alone in this journey. By addressing both physical and emotional challenges with compassion and determination, you can create a sustainable path to better health.

SCIENTIFIC BENEFITS OF LOSING WEIGHT

Embarking on a weight loss journey is not just about shedding pounds; it's about embracing a multitude of **scientific benefits** that enhance both your physical and mental well-being. As you navigate through the 1200-calorie diet plan, you'll discover how losing weight can significantly improve your **health** and quality of life.

First and foremost, reducing excess weight can lead to **lower blood pressure**, which is crucial for maintaining heart health. By alleviating the strain on your cardiovascular system, you reduce the risk of heart disease and stroke, paving the way for a longer, healthier life.

Weight loss also plays a vital role in **regulating blood sugar levels**. For individuals at risk of or living with diabetes, achieving a healthier weight can improve insulin sensitivity, making it easier to manage blood sugar and reduce the need for medication.

Beyond physical health, shedding pounds can boost your **mental well-being**. As your body becomes more agile, you'll likely experience increased energy and confidence, which can lead to improved self-esteem and a more positive outlook on life.

Additionally, losing weight can alleviate pressure on **joints**, reducing pain and improving mobility. This newfound freedom can enhance your ability to engage in physical activities, further supporting your weight loss journey.

Ultimately, the scientific benefits of weight loss extend far beyond the scale, offering profound improvements to your overall health and happiness.

HOW 1200 CALORIES MAKE A DIFFERENCE

Embarking on a journey with a **1200-calorie diet** might seem daunting at first, but understanding its impact can be the key to unlocking a healthier, more vibrant life. Many people ask, "Why 1200 calories?" The answer lies in its ability to create a **caloric deficit** that promotes weight loss while still providing the essential nutrients your body needs.

Imagine your body as a finely tuned machine. Just like any machine, it requires the right amount of fuel to function optimally. By consuming 1200 calories, you're giving your body just enough to sustain energy and maintain vital processes without excess. This balance is crucial for those seeking to shed pounds without feeling deprived or fatigued.

One of the most profound benefits of this diet is the **boost in energy levels**. Initially, you might expect to feel sluggish with fewer calories, but many find the opposite to be true. By focusing on nutrient-dense foods, you provide your body with high-quality fuel, leading to increased energy and productivity throughout the day.

Moreover, the **psychological benefits** cannot be overstated. As you begin to see and feel the changes in your body, your confidence and self-esteem will naturally rise. This newfound positivity can have a ripple effect, improving relationships and personal outlook.

Finally, the 1200-calorie plan is designed to be **inclusive and adaptable**. Whether you're cooking for yourself or feeding a family, the recipes and strategies can fit seamlessly into your lifestyle, making it easier to stick with and enjoy the journey to better health.

Understanding Caloric Deficits

Embarking on a journey towards healthier living often begins with understanding the concept of a **caloric deficit**. At its core, a caloric deficit occurs when you consume fewer calories than your body needs to maintain its current weight. This is the cornerstone of any effective weight loss strategy, as it prompts your body to tap into stored energy reserves, leading to fat loss.

Imagine your body as a finely tuned machine. It requires a certain amount of fuel—calories—to function optimally. When you provide it with fewer calories, it begins to use its stored energy, much like a car using its reserve fuel tank. The key is finding the right balance: enough of a deficit to promote weight loss, but not so extreme that it leads to fatigue or nutritional deficiencies.

It's important to remember that achieving a caloric deficit doesn't mean deprivation. Instead, it's about making **smart food choices** that fill you up without overloading your calorie intake. Think of nutrient-dense foods like fruits, vegetables, lean proteins, and whole grains. These foods not only support your body's needs but also help you feel satisfied and energized throughout the day.

As you navigate this path, be mindful of your body's signals. Hunger, energy levels, and mood can all provide valuable feedback. By listening to your body and making informed choices, you can maintain a caloric deficit that is both **sustainable and effective** for your weight loss goals.

Why This Calorie Count is Effective for Rapid, Safe Weight Loss

Embarking on a weight loss journey can often feel like navigating a maze of conflicting advice and overwhelming options. Yet, the essence of effective weight loss lies in simplicity and science. A **1200-calorie diet** offers a balanced approach, providing enough energy to sustain your body while creating a caloric deficit essential for shedding pounds. This method is not only about cutting calories but about making every calorie count.

Imagine your body as a finely tuned machine. To operate optimally, it requires fuel—nutrients that empower you to function throughout the day. By focusing on nutrient-dense foods within a 1200-calorie framework, you ensure your body receives the **vitamins, minerals, and energy** it needs without excess. This balance is key to avoiding the pitfalls of fatigue and nutrient deficiency that often accompany more restrictive diets.

Moreover, this diet plan is designed to be **sustainable**. It encourages you to adopt eating habits that are not only effective in the short term but also maintainable in the long run. By developing a deeper understanding of portion control and food choices, you pave the way for a healthier lifestyle that extends beyond the confines of a diet.

Adhering to a 1200-calorie plan requires **mindfulness and commitment**, but the rewards are worth the effort. As you progress, you'll notice not just a change in the numbers on the scale, but a transformation in your energy levels, confidence, and overall well-being. Embrace this journey with optimism, knowing that each step brings you closer to reclaiming your health and vitality.

CHAPTER 2: GETTING STARTED

Embarking on a journey towards a healthier lifestyle can feel daunting, yet it begins with a single, decisive step. Imagine standing at the edge of a vast forest, the path to a healthier you winding through the trees. This path, while challenging, is navigable with the right tools and mindset. **Mindset** is crucial; it transforms obstacles into opportunities and setbacks into lessons.

As you dive into the 1200-calorie diet plan, consider it not as a restriction, but as a **liberation** from habits that no longer serve you. Picture your kitchen as a lab of possibilities, where each ingredient is a building block for your new life. Start with small, consistent changes. Swap processed snacks for vibrant fruits, and sugary drinks for refreshing water infused with lemon or mint. These swaps, though simple, are powerful.

Visualize your day as a tapestry woven with moments of mindful eating. Enjoy each meal, savoring the flavors and textures. This practice not only enhances your dining experience but also fosters a deeper connection with your body's needs. Remember, **progress** is personal and non-linear. Celebrate every victory, no matter how small, and learn from every challenge.

Your journey is unique, and while others may walk alongside you, your path is yours alone. Embrace this transformation with an open heart and a determined spirit. With each step, you're not just losing weight; you're gaining a **healthier, happier** life.

SETTING REALISTIC GOALS

Embarking on a journey toward better health starts with setting **realistic goals**. These goals are not just about the numbers on the scale but about creating a sustainable lifestyle that enhances your overall well-being. Begin by reflecting on what you truly want to achieve and why it matters to you. This personal clarity will serve as your compass, guiding you through challenges and keeping you motivated.

It's crucial to set **achievable milestones** that celebrate progress, no matter how small. For instance, instead of aiming to lose a large amount of weight in a short time, focus on losing a few pounds each month. This approach not only prevents burnout but also encourages a positive relationship with your body and your journey.

Consider incorporating **non-scale victories** into your goals. These could be as simple as having more energy to play with your kids, fitting into a favorite pair of jeans, or feeling more confident in social settings. Recognizing these achievements reinforces the idea that health is about more than just weight loss.

Remember, your goals should be **flexible**. Life can be unpredictable, and it's okay to adjust your expectations as needed. The key is to remain committed to your overarching vision of a healthier, more fulfilling life. By setting realistic goals, you lay the foundation for lasting change, empowering yourself to reclaim your health and vitality.

HOW TO MEASURE SUCCESS BEYOND THE SCALE

Embarking on a weight loss journey often brings the focus to numbers on a scale. Yet, true success reaches far beyond these digits. It's vital to recognize the myriad of other ways to measure progress and celebrate victories that aren't quantified by weight alone.

Consider the **energy boost** you experience as you embrace healthier habits. Suddenly, tasks that once seemed daunting become manageable, and you find yourself more engaged in daily activities. This newfound vitality is a clear indicator of your body's positive response to the changes you're implementing.

Another marker of success is the **improvement in self-esteem**. As you commit to your health goals, you may notice a shift in how you perceive yourself. Confidence grows not from the numbers on the scale, but from the dedication and resilience you demonstrate every day.

Pay attention to the **quality of sleep**. A balanced diet and regular activity often lead to more restful nights, ensuring you wake up refreshed and ready to tackle the day. This improvement is a testament to your body's internal alignment with your health efforts.

Finally, observe the **positive changes in your relationships**. As you prioritize your well-being, you may find yourself more present and connected with loved ones, fostering deeper bonds and shared moments of joy.

Understanding Your Caloric Needs

Embarking on a journey towards better health begins with understanding your **caloric needs**. This essential knowledge serves as the foundation for effective weight management and overall well-being. Calories are the units of energy that fuel our bodies, and knowing how much energy you need is crucial for crafting a diet plan that supports your goals.

Determining your daily caloric requirement involves considering several factors, such as your **age**, **gender**, **weight**, **height**, and **activity level**. These elements collectively influence your Basal Metabolic Rate (BMR), which is the number of calories your body needs at rest to maintain vital functions like breathing and circulation.

To calculate your BMR, you can use various formulas, such as the **Harris-Benedict equation**. Once you have your BMR, it's time to factor in your physical activity. Whether you lead a sedentary lifestyle or are regularly active, adjusting your caloric intake to match your activity level is key to achieving your weight loss objectives.

Remember, the goal is to create a **caloric deficit**, where you consume fewer calories than your body needs to maintain its current weight. This deficit encourages your body to utilize stored fat for energy, leading to gradual, sustainable weight loss.

Understanding your caloric needs empowers you to make informed choices, paving the way for a healthier, more vibrant life. With this knowledge, you're equipped to tailor your diet to your unique requirements, ensuring both effectiveness and sustainability.

Adapting the 1200-Calorie Plan to Your Body

Embarking on a 1200-calorie diet doesn't mean a one-size-fits-all approach. It's about **listening to your body** and making adjustments that align with your unique needs. Start by understanding your **metabolic rate**—the energy your body uses at rest. This will help you gauge how your body responds to the calorie intake and ensure you're not depriving it of essential nutrients.

Pay attention to your **hunger signals**. If you find yourself feeling excessively hungry, it might be your body's way of telling you it needs more fuel, especially if you're engaging in regular physical activity. In such cases, consider incorporating nutrient-dense, low-calorie foods like leafy greens or lean proteins to keep your energy levels stable.

Remember, **hydration** plays a crucial role in how your body processes calories. Often, what feels like hunger is actually thirst. Drinking enough water can aid digestion and help manage your appetite.

Finally, be mindful of your **emotional state**. Emotional eating can sabotage your efforts. Instead of reaching for food when stressed, try alternative stress-relief methods like meditation or a short walk. By personalizing your plan, you'll be better equipped to navigate challenges and maintain your commitment to a healthier lifestyle.

TOOLS FOR SUCCESS

Embarking on the journey to transform your health requires not just a plan but a toolkit of resources to ensure success. Imagine setting sail on a voyage; you wouldn't leave the dock without the right equipment. Similarly, in your pursuit of weight loss, having the right tools can make all the difference.

First, let's talk about the **importance of preparation**. Before diving into the 1200-calorie diet, take time to **organize your kitchen**. Stock your pantry with essentials like whole grains, lean proteins, and fresh vegetables. Having these items readily available will help you avoid the temptation of unhealthy alternatives.

Next, consider the role of **meal planning**. By dedicating a few hours each week to plan your meals, you can ensure a balanced intake of nutrients while sticking to your calorie goals. Use a food journal or an app to track your progress, making adjustments as needed.

Support is another crucial tool. Whether it's a friend, family member, or online community, having a **support network** can provide encouragement and accountability. Share your goals and celebrate successes together, creating a positive environment for growth.

Lastly, remember the power of **mindfulness**. Being present during meals, savoring each bite, and listening to your body's hunger cues can transform your relationship with food. This mindful approach fosters a deeper connection with your health journey, paving the way for lasting change.

WHAT YOU'LL NEED: SCALES, MEAL PREP CONTAINERS, AND MORE

Embarking on a transformative journey towards better health requires not just commitment but also the right tools. As you dive into Dr. Now's 1200-Calorie Diet Plan, you'll find that having a few essential items on hand can make all the difference. Let's explore what you'll need to set yourself up for success.

First, a reliable **kitchen scale** is indispensable. Accurately measuring your portions is crucial when adhering to a calorie-restricted diet. This tool helps ensure you're consuming the right amounts, preventing unintentional overindulgence. Remember, precision in portion sizes can significantly impact your progress.

Next, consider investing in quality **meal prep containers**. These containers are not only practical for organizing your meals but also serve as a visual reminder of your commitment to this journey. Preparing meals in advance can save time, reduce stress, and help you avoid the temptation of unhealthy options when hunger strikes.

Another helpful addition is a **food journal**. Documenting your meals, emotions, and progress can provide valuable insights into your eating habits and triggers. This practice fosters mindfulness and accountability, allowing you to track patterns and make informed adjustments.

Lastly, a **supportive community**—whether online or in-person—can provide encouragement and shared experiences. Connecting with others on a similar path can bolster your resolve and offer fresh perspectives on overcoming challenges.

With these tools in your arsenal, you're well-equipped to navigate the rewarding path towards improved health and vitality. Remember, each step you take is a testament to your strength and determination.

How to Use This Book Effectively

Welcome to a journey toward a healthier, more vibrant you. This book is designed to be your trusted companion, guiding you through the complexities of weight loss with empathy and clarity. As you dive into these pages, you'll discover **practical strategies** and **motivational stories** that aim to make your journey both manageable and inspiring.

To get the most out of this book, approach it with an open mind and a willingness to embrace change. Begin by setting **realistic goals** that align with your personal needs and lifestyle. Remember, this is not just about shedding pounds but about fostering a sustainable, healthy way of living.

Engage actively with the content by reflecting on the **real-world examples** and anecdotes shared here. Let them serve as reminders that you're not alone in this journey. As you progress, revisit sections that resonate with you, and apply the advice to your daily routine.

Lastly, trust in the process and in yourself. This book is your ally, offering **supportive guidance** every step of the way. Embrace each chapter as a stepping stone toward reclaiming your health and confidence.

CHAPTER 3: MEAL PLANNING MADE SIMPLE

Imagine waking up each morning with a sense of excitement, knowing that your meals for the day are not only delicious but also aligned with your health goals. This is the power of **effective meal planning**. It transforms what might feel like a daunting task into a creative, empowering journey.

Think of meal planning as a canvas where you can paint your path to health. It's not about restriction, but rather about **freedom**—freedom to choose meals that satisfy both your taste buds and your nutritional needs. The key lies in **simplicity**. Start by envisioning your favorite dishes and then reimagining them in a healthier light. Perhaps you love a hearty lasagna; consider a version with zucchini noodles and lean turkey. The possibilities are endless.

One of my favorite stories is of a reader who found joy in preparing meals with her children. They turned meal prep into a family affair, making it not only a healthful endeavor but also a bonding experience. The laughter and lessons learned in the kitchen became as nourishing as the meals themselves. This is the essence of meal planning—it's about **connection**, with your food, your family, and your goals.

Remember, the journey to a healthier you is a marathon, not a sprint. Each meal planned is a step towards reclaiming your health and vitality. Embrace it with an open heart and a curious mind.

STRUCTURING YOUR DAY

Incorporating a **structured routine** into your daily life can be a transformative step on your journey to better health. It's not just about sticking to a diet; it's about **creating a lifestyle** that supports your goals. Start each day with a **clear plan**—this sets the tone for success. Begin with a nourishing breakfast, ensuring it's both **balanced and satisfying**. This will help curb cravings and provide the energy you need to tackle the day.

Mid-morning, take a moment to **reassess your goals** and remind yourself why you embarked on this journey. This is your time to reflect and recalibrate if necessary. Engage in a brief physical activity, whether it's a walk around the block or a quick stretch, to keep your energy levels up.

Lunch should be a time of **mindful eating**. Focus on your meal, savoring each bite, and avoid distractions like screens or work. This practice not only enhances digestion but also helps in recognizing satiety signals.

As the afternoon progresses, it's common to experience a dip in energy. Combat this by incorporating a healthy snack that aligns with your **caloric goals**. It might be a handful of nuts or a piece of fruit—something that will provide a **nutritional boost** without derailing your plan.

Evenings are a crucial time for **relaxation and reflection**. Dedicate time to unwind, whether through meditation, reading, or a calming hobby. This not only aids in stress management but also prepares your body for a restful night's sleep, which is vital for **overall well-being**.

Remember, consistency is key. By structuring your day with intention and purpose, you're not just following a diet; you're laying the foundation for a healthier, more fulfilling life.

HOW TO BALANCE MEALS FOR ENERGY AND SATISFACTION

Balancing meals for energy and satisfaction is all about understanding the **right combination** of nutrients. A well-balanced meal should include a mix of **proteins, carbohydrates, and healthy fats**. These components work together to keep you satisfied and energized throughout the day.

Start by focusing on **portion control**. It's not just about what you eat, but how much. Aim to fill half your plate with **vegetables**, a quarter with **lean protein**, and the remaining quarter with **whole grains**. This simple formula ensures you're getting a variety of nutrients without overindulging.

Protein is crucial for maintaining muscle mass and keeping hunger at bay. Incorporate sources like **chicken, fish, beans, or tofu** into your meals. Carbohydrates are your body's main energy source, so choose **complex carbs** like brown rice, quinoa, or whole-grain bread, which provide sustained energy.

Don't forget about **healthy fats**. They play a vital role in brain function and hormone production. Add small amounts of **avocado, nuts, or olive oil** to your meals for a boost of flavor and nutrition.

Lastly, listen to your body. Eating mindfully and recognizing when you're **truly hungry** or full can help you make better food choices and maintain balance in your diet.

MEAL FREQUENCY: 3 MAIN MEALS + 1 SNACK

In the journey to reclaiming your health, understanding how to structure your meals is crucial. With the **3 main meals and 1 snack** approach, you're not just eating to lose weight, but to nourish your body and fuel your day. This method provides a balance that keeps you satisfied, reduces cravings, and supports your metabolism.

Start your day with a **nutritious breakfast**, setting the tone for sustained energy. Think of it as your morning ritual, a time to enjoy the flavors and textures that kickstart your metabolism. Opt for options like oatmeal with fresh fruit or a veggie omelet, which are both satisfying and nutrient-dense.

Come midday, your **lunch** should be a hearty mix of lean proteins and colorful vegetables. This combination not only fuels your afternoon but also keeps your energy levels steady. Consider a grilled chicken salad or a quinoa bowl with mixed greens and beans.

As the day winds down, your **dinner** is a chance to unwind with a meal that comforts but doesn't compromise your goals. Think baked salmon with steamed broccoli or a stir-fry with tofu and mixed veggies. The key is to keep it light yet fulfilling.

Finally, allow yourself a **snack** that satisfies your taste buds without derailing your progress. A handful of nuts, a piece of fruit, or some yogurt can be the perfect end to your day.

SHOPPING MADE EASY

Embarking on a journey of health transformation begins right at the grocery store. It's the place where your choices set the stage for success. But fear not—shopping for a 1200-calorie diet doesn't have to be overwhelming. With a bit of planning and mindfulness, you can turn this task into an empowering experience.

First, let's talk about **preparation**. Before stepping foot in the store, take a moment to plan your meals for the week. This not only saves time but also keeps you focused on purchasing only what you need. Make a list and stick to it. This simple step can help you avoid those tempting aisles filled with high-calorie snacks.

As you navigate the aisles, focus on the perimeter of the store. Here, you'll find fresh produce, lean proteins, and dairy—staples of a balanced diet. Opt for whole foods that are as close to their natural state as possible. Think **colorful vegetables**, **lean meats**, and whole grains. These foods are not only nutrient-dense but also satisfying, helping you stay full while adhering to your calorie goals.

Consider exploring the bulk section for staples like brown rice, quinoa, and nuts. Buying in bulk can be a **cost-effective** strategy, allowing you to purchase exactly what you need without overspending.

Finally, don't forget to read labels. Understanding nutritional information empowers you to make informed decisions, ensuring that each item supports your health goals. Remember, shopping is the first step toward reclaiming your life and health. With each thoughtful choice, you're one step closer to a healthier, more vibrant you.

BUDGET-FRIENDLY GROCERY LISTS

Embarking on a 1200-calorie diet doesn't mean sacrificing flavor or breaking the bank. With a little planning and creativity, you can enjoy a variety of delicious meals without overspending. Let's explore how to make the most of your grocery budget while sticking to your dietary goals.

First, focus on **whole foods**. Not only are they often more affordable, but they also pack a nutritional punch. Opt for seasonal fruits and vegetables, which tend to be less expensive and fresher. Think of staples like carrots, apples, and leafy greens. These ingredients are versatile and can be used in numerous recipes.

Next, consider **buying in bulk** where possible. Items like oats, brown rice, and beans are cost-effective and provide great nutritional value. They're perfect for creating hearty, satisfying meals that keep you full longer. Remember, a little goes a long way with these ingredients.

Don't overlook the power of **frozen produce**. It's a budget-friendly alternative to fresh produce and retains most of its nutrients. Frozen berries, spinach, and mixed vegetables can be lifesavers when fresh options are pricey or unavailable.

Lastly, plan your meals around **affordable proteins** such as eggs, lentils, and chicken thighs. These options are not only cost-effective but also provide essential nutrients to support your health journey.

By prioritizing these strategies, you can enjoy a diverse, satisfying diet while staying within your budget. Remember, every small step you take brings you closer to reclaiming your health and vitality.

ESSENTIAL PANTRY STAPLES

As you embark on the journey towards a healthier lifestyle, having a well-stocked pantry can make all the difference. The right ingredients not only simplify meal preparation but also ensure you stay on track with your **1200-calorie diet plan**. Let's explore some essential pantry staples that will support your weight loss goals while keeping your meals both nutritious and satisfying.

First, consider incorporating a variety of **whole grains** such as quinoa, brown rice, and oats. These grains are rich in fiber, which helps keep you full and satisfied. They also provide a steady release of energy, making them a perfect base for many meals.

Next, stock up on **lean proteins** like canned tuna, beans, and lentils. These options are not only affordable but also versatile, allowing you to create a range of dishes from salads to hearty stews. Lean proteins are crucial for maintaining muscle mass while losing weight.

Don't forget to include a selection of **healthy fats** such as olive oil, nuts, and seeds. These fats are essential for overall health and can enhance the flavor of your meals. Just remember to use them in moderation to stay within your calorie limits.

Finally, keep a variety of **spices and herbs** on hand. They can transform simple dishes into flavorful creations without adding extra calories. Experiment with different combinations to keep your meals exciting and enjoyable.

By filling your pantry with these staples, you'll be well-equipped to tackle your weight loss journey with confidence and ease. Remember, preparation is key to success, and a thoughtfully stocked pantry is your first step towards achieving your health goals.

Weekly Meal Plans

Embarking on a journey to better health and well-being begins with a well-structured meal plan. The cornerstone of our approach is simplicity and **sustainability**. Each week, you'll find a carefully curated plan that not only aligns with the 1200-calorie framework but also caters to your taste buds and daily routine.

Week one is about **familiarizing** yourself with new flavors and textures, introducing a variety of foods that nourish both body and soul. Start your day with a hearty breakfast like oatmeal topped with fresh berries, providing the energy and satisfaction needed to tackle the morning. For lunch, a colorful salad with lean proteins ensures you're fueled and focused through the afternoon. Dinner is a chance to unwind with a delicious, balanced meal such as grilled chicken with steamed vegetables.

As you progress, the meal plans evolve to keep you engaged and motivated. You'll notice a **gradual shift** towards more complex recipes, incorporating diverse ingredients that keep your palate excited. Snacks are strategically placed to stave off hunger and maintain energy levels, featuring options like nuts, yogurt, or fruit.

Remember, the goal is not just weight loss but a **holistic transformation**. Embrace this plan with an open mind and a hopeful heart, knowing that each meal is a step towards a healthier, more vibrant you.

Sample Menus for Week 1 and Beyond

Embarking on the first week of the **Dr. Now 1200-Calorie Diet Plan** can feel like stepping into uncharted territory. Yet, with a clear menu and a dash of determination, you're setting the stage for transformative change. As you navigate this journey, remember that each meal is not just about nourishment but a step towards reclaiming your health.

Start your day with a breakfast that fuels your body and mind. Consider a **hearty bowl of oatmeal** topped with fresh berries. It's a simple, satisfying choice that provides a slow release of energy, keeping you satiated until lunch.

For lunch, a **colorful salad** loaded with mixed greens, cherry tomatoes, and lean protein like grilled chicken or chickpeas offers a refreshing, nutrient-dense meal. Drizzle with a light vinaigrette to enhance flavors without adding unnecessary calories.

As dinner approaches, opt for a **balanced plate** featuring a small portion of whole grains, such as quinoa or brown rice, paired with steamed vegetables and a serving of fish or tofu. This combination supports your body's needs while keeping your calorie count in check.

Snacks can be a bridge between meals. Choose wisely with options like a handful of almonds or a piece of fruit. Remember, the goal is to maintain energy levels without exceeding your calorie limit.

Throughout the week, listen to your body's signals. Adjust portions if needed, and stay hydrated with plenty of water. This plan is not just about restriction; it's about making choices that empower you to live a healthier, more fulfilling life.

CHAPTER 4: RECIPES FOR EVERY OCCASION

Imagine hosting a dinner party where every dish is not only delicious but also aligns with your **1200-calorie diet plan**. This chapter will guide you through creating meals that are as enjoyable to eat as they are beneficial for your health. Whether it's a cozy family gathering or a festive celebration, these recipes are crafted to fit seamlessly into your lifestyle.

Let's start with a **hearty breakfast** that fuels your day. Consider a veggie-packed omelet, bursting with colors and flavors, paired with a refreshing side of mixed berries. This combination not only satisfies your taste buds but also keeps you energized throughout the morning.

For lunch, a **zesty quinoa salad** with cherry tomatoes, cucumbers, and a sprinkle of feta cheese offers a delightful crunch and a wealth of nutrients. Drizzle with a light lemon vinaigrette to enhance the flavors without adding unnecessary calories.

As the day winds down, a **grilled salmon** dinner, accompanied by steamed asparagus and a quinoa pilaf, promises a satisfying end. The rich omega-3s in salmon support heart health, while the vibrant greens and grains provide essential vitamins and minerals.

Remember, each meal is an opportunity to nourish your body and soul. With these recipes, you can relish every occasion, knowing you're making choices that support your **health journey** and bring you closer to your goals.

BREAKFASTS

QUINOA AND CHIA SEED PORRIDGE

PREPARATION TIME: 5 min - **COOKING TIME:** 20 min

MODE OF COOKING: Simmering - **SERVINGS:** 2

INGREDIENTS:

- 1/2 cup quinoa, rinsed
- 1 1/2 cups almond milk
- 1 Tbsp chia seeds
- 1 tsp vanilla extract
- 1/2 tsp ground cinnamon
- 1 Tbsp maple syrup
- Fresh berries for topping
- Pinch of salt

DIRECTIONS:

- In a saucepan, combine quinoa, almond milk, chia seeds, vanilla extract, cinnamon, and salt.

- Bring to a gentle simmer over medium heat, stirring occasionally.

- Reduce heat to low, cover, and let simmer for 15-20 minutes until quinoa is tender and the mixture is creamy.

- Stir in maple syrup and serve topped with fresh berries.

TIPS:

- Add a dollop of Greek yogurt for extra creaminess.

- Sprinkle with toasted nuts for added crunch.

N.V.: Calories: 250, Fat: 7g, Carbs: 40g, Protein: 7g, Sugar: 12g

AVOCADO AND SMOKED SALMON TOAST

PREPARATION TIME: 10 min - **COOKING TIME:** 0 min

MODE OF COOKING: No Cooking - **SERVINGS:** 2

INGREDIENTS:

- 2 slices whole-grain bread, toasted

- 1 ripe avocado

- 2 oz smoked salmon

- 1 Tbsp capers

- 1/2 lemon, juiced

- Fresh dill for garnish

- Salt and pepper to taste

DIRECTIONS:

- Mash the avocado in a bowl with lemon juice, salt, and pepper.

- Spread the avocado mixture evenly over the toasted bread slices.

- Top with slices of smoked salmon and sprinkle with capers.
- Garnish with fresh dill before serving.

TIPS:

- Use gluten-free bread for a celiac-friendly option.
- Add thinly sliced red onion for extra flavor.

N.V.: Calories: 300, Fat: 18g, Carbs: 26g, Protein: 12g, Sugar: 2g

SWEET POTATO AND BLACK BEAN BREAKFAST HASH

PREPARATION TIME: 10 min - **COOKING TIME:** 25 min

MODE OF COOKING: Sautéing - **SERVINGS:** 2

INGREDIENTS:

- 1 large sweet potato, peeled and diced
- 1 Tbsp olive oil
- 1/2 cup black beans, rinsed and drained
- 1/2 red bell pepper, diced
- 1/4 cup red onion, chopped
- 1 tsp smoked paprika
- 1/2 tsp cumin
- Salt and pepper to taste
- Fresh cilantro for garnish

DIRECTIONS:

- Heat olive oil in a large skillet over medium heat.
- Add sweet potatoes and cook until they begin to soften, about 10 minutes.
- Add bell pepper, onion, smoked paprika, and cumin, cooking for an additional 10 minutes.
- Stir in black beans and cook until heated through.

- Season with salt and pepper, garnish with cilantro, and serve.

TIPS:

- Top with a poached egg for added protein.
- Serve with a side of salsa for extra flavor.

N.V.: Calories: 200, Fat: 7g, Carbs: 32g, Protein: 5g, Sugar: 6g

SPINACH AND FETA OMELETTE

PREPARATION TIME: 5 min - **COOKING TIME:** 10 min

MODE OF COOKING: Frying - **SERVINGS:** 1

INGREDIENTS:

- 2 large eggs
- 1/4 cup fresh spinach, chopped
- 2 Tbsp feta cheese, crumbled
- 1 Tbsp milk
- 1 tsp olive oil
- Salt and pepper to taste

DIRECTIONS:

- Whisk eggs with milk, salt, and pepper in a bowl.
- Heat olive oil in a non-stick skillet over medium heat.
- Pour in the egg mixture and cook until edges begin to set.
- Sprinkle spinach and feta over half of the omelette.
- Fold the omelette in half and cook for 1-2 more minutes until cheese melts.

TIPS:

- Add sun-dried tomatoes for a Mediterranean twist.
- Use goat cheese for a creamier texture.

N.V.: Calories: 220, Fat: 17g, Carbs: 2g, Protein: 14g, Sugar: 1g

OVERNIGHT OATS WITH APPLE AND CINNAMON

PREPARATION TIME: 5 min - **COOKING TIME:** 0 min

MODE OF COOKING: No Cooking - **SERVINGS:** 1

INGREDIENTS:

- 1/2 cup rolled oats
- 1/2 cup unsweetened almond milk
- 1/4 cup unsweetened applesauce
- 1/2 tsp ground cinnamon
- 1 Tbsp chopped walnuts
- 1 tsp honey
- 1/4 apple, thinly sliced

DIRECTIONS:

- Combine oats, almond milk, applesauce, and cinnamon in a jar or bowl.
- Stir well, cover, and refrigerate overnight.
- In the morning, stir again and top with walnuts, honey, and apple slices before serving.

TIPS:

- Use steel-cut oats for a chewier texture.
- Add a pinch of nutmeg for extra warmth.

N.V.: Calories: 300, Fat: 10g, Carbs: 47g, Protein: 6g, Sugar: 14g

ZUCCHINI AND TOMATO FRITTATA

PREPARATION TIME: 10 min - **COOKING TIME:** 20 min

MODE OF COOKING: Baking - **SERVINGS:** 4

INGREDIENTS:

- 1 medium zucchini, sliced
- 1 cup cherry tomatoes, halved
- 6 large eggs
- 1/4 cup milk
- 1/4 cup Parmesan cheese, grated
- 1 Tbsp olive oil
- Salt and pepper to taste

DIRECTIONS:

- Preheat oven to 375°F (190°C).
- In a skillet, heat olive oil over medium heat and sauté zucchini until softened.
- Add tomatoes and cook for another 2 minutes.
- Whisk eggs, milk, Parmesan, salt, and pepper in a bowl.
- Pour egg mixture over vegetables in the skillet.
- Transfer skillet to oven and bake for 15 minutes or until the frittata is set.

TIPS:

- Use a cast-iron skillet for even cooking.
- Garnish with fresh basil for added aroma.

N.V.: Calories: 180, Fat: 12g, Carbs: 6g, Protein: 12g, Sugar: 3g

BANANA AND ALMOND BUTTER SMOOTHIE

PREPARATION TIME: 5 min - **COOKING TIME:** 0 min

MODE OF COOKING: Blending - **SERVINGS:** 1

INGREDIENTS:

- 1 ripe banana

- 1 Tbsp almond butter
- 1 cup unsweetened almond milk
- 1 tsp chia seeds
- 1/2 tsp vanilla extract
- Ice cubes (optional)

DIRECTIONS:

- Combine banana, almond butter, almond milk, chia seeds, and vanilla extract in a blender.
- Blend until smooth and creamy.
- Add ice cubes and blend again if a colder, thicker consistency is desired.

TIPS:

- Substitute almond butter with peanut butter for a different flavor.
- Add a handful of spinach for a nutrient boost.

N.V.: Calories: 250, Fat: 10g, Carbs: 35g, Protein: 5g, Sugar: 15g

WHOLE WHEAT PANCAKES WITH BERRIES

PREPARATION TIME: 10 min - **COOKING TIME:** 15 min

MODE OF COOKING: Griddling - **SERVINGS:** 4

INGREDIENTS:

- 1 cup whole wheat flour
- 1 Tbsp baking powder
- 1/2 tsp salt
- 1 cup skim milk
- 1 large egg
- 2 Tbsp honey
- 1 tsp vanilla extract

- Fresh mixed berries for topping
- Cooking spray

DIRECTIONS:

- In a bowl, mix flour, baking powder, and salt.
- In another bowl, whisk milk, egg, honey, and vanilla extract.
- Combine wet and dry ingredients, stirring until just mixed.
- Heat a griddle over medium heat and coat with cooking spray.
- Pour 1/4 cup batter for each pancake and cook until bubbles form on the surface.
- Flip and cook until golden brown. Serve with fresh berries.

TIPS:

- Use buttermilk for a tangier taste.
- Top with a dollop of Greek yogurt for extra protein.

N.V.: Calories: 200, Fat: 3g, Carbs: 38g, Protein: 7g, Sugar: 10g

ENERGIZING OPTIONS TO START YOUR DAY

Starting your day with the right fuel is crucial for setting the tone for successful weight management and overall well-being. Breakfast doesn't have to be complicated or time-consuming. It should be about making choices that are both **nourishing** and **energizing**, setting you up for a productive day.

Consider beginning with a **protein-rich** option. A simple scramble with egg whites and spinach not only provides essential nutrients but also keeps you feeling full longer, reducing the temptation to snack before lunch. Pair it with a slice of whole-grain toast for added fiber and energy.

If you're short on time, a **smoothie** can be a quick and nutritious choice. Blend a mix of your favorite fruits, a handful of greens, and a scoop of protein powder. This combination ensures you get a balance of vitamins, minerals, and protein, all in one convenient glass.

For those who enjoy something sweet, oatmeal can be a versatile option. Top it with fresh berries and a sprinkle of nuts for a satisfying breakfast that's both **heart-healthy** and delicious. Remember, the goal is to create a meal that not only fuels your body but also brings a sense of joy and satisfaction to your morning routine.

LUNCHES

QUINOA-STUFFED BELL PEPPERS

PREPARATION TIME: 20 min - **COOKING TIME:** 35 min

MODE OF COOKING: Baking - **SERVINGS:** 4

INGREDIENTS:

- 4 large bell peppers, tops removed and seeds cleaned
- 1 cup quinoa, rinsed
- 2 cups vegetable broth
- 1 cup cherry tomatoes, halved
- 1/2 cup black beans, drained and rinsed
- 1/4 cup chopped fresh cilantro
- 1 tsp cumin powder
- 1 tsp smoked paprika
- Salt and pepper to taste
- 1 Tbsp olive oil
- Juice of 1 lime

DIRECTIONS:

- Preheat oven to 375°F (190°C).
- In a saucepan, combine quinoa and vegetable broth. Bring to a boil, then reduce heat to low, cover, and simmer until liquid is absorbed, about 15 min.
- In a bowl, mix cooked quinoa, cherry tomatoes, black beans, cilantro, cumin, smoked paprika, salt, and pepper.
- Stuff each bell pepper with the quinoa mixture. Drizzle olive oil over the top.
- Place stuffed peppers in a baking dish and bake for 35 min until peppers are tender.
- Squeeze lime juice over the peppers before serving.

TIPS:

- Top with avocado slices for added creaminess.
- Serve with a side salad for a complete meal.

N.V.: Calories: 240, Fat: 5g, Carbs: 40g, Protein: 8g, Sugar: 6g

SPICY LENTIL AND SWEET POTATO STEW

PREPARATION TIME: 15 min - **COOKING TIME:** 40 min

MODE OF COOKING: Simmering - **SERVINGS:** 4

INGREDIENTS:

- 1 cup red lentils, rinsed
- 2 medium sweet potatoes, peeled and diced
- 1 onion, chopped
- 3 cloves garlic, minced
- 1 Tbsp ginger, grated
- 1 tsp turmeric powder
- 1 tsp cayenne pepper
- 4 cups vegetable broth
- 1 can (14 oz) coconut milk
- 2 Tbsp olive oil
- Salt and pepper to taste
- Fresh cilantro for garnish

DIRECTIONS:

- Heat olive oil in a large pot over medium heat. Sauté onion, garlic, and ginger until onion is translucent.
- Add turmeric and cayenne pepper, stirring for 1 min until fragrant.
- Stir in sweet potatoes and lentils, then add vegetable broth. Bring to a boil.

- Reduce heat to low, cover, and simmer for 30 min until sweet potatoes are tender.
- Stir in coconut milk, season with salt and pepper, and simmer for an additional 5 min.
- Garnish with fresh cilantro before serving.

TIPS:

- Serve with crusty bread for dipping.
- Adjust cayenne pepper to taste for desired heat level.

N.V.: Calories: 310, Fat: 12g, Carbs: 45g, Protein: 10g, Sugar: 8g

CHICKPEA AND AVOCADO SALAD WRAP

PREPARATION TIME: 15 min - **COOKING TIME:** 0 min

MODE OF COOKING: No cooking - **SERVINGS:** 4

INGREDIENTS:

- 1 can (15 oz) chickpeas, drained and rinsed
- 2 ripe avocados, peeled and pitted
- 1/4 cup red onion, finely chopped
- 1/4 cup fresh parsley, chopped
- Juice of 1 lemon
- Salt and pepper to taste
- 4 large whole-grain wraps
- 2 cups mixed greens

DIRECTIONS:

- In a bowl, mash chickpeas and avocados together until slightly chunky.
- Mix in red onion, parsley, lemon juice, salt, and pepper.
- Lay wraps flat and spread chickpea mixture evenly across each one.
- Top with mixed greens, roll up tightly, and slice in half before serving.

TIPS:

- Add sliced radishes for extra crunch.
- Use gluten-free wraps if needed.

N.V.: Calories: 340, Fat: 18g, Carbs: 40g, Protein: 9g, Sugar: 3g

GRILLED EGGPLANT AND TOMATO STACK

PREPARATION TIME: 10 min - **COOKING TIME:** 15 min

MODE OF COOKING: Grilling - **SERVINGS:** 4

INGREDIENTS:

- 2 medium eggplants, sliced into 1/2-inch rounds
- 3 large tomatoes, sliced
- 1/4 cup balsamic vinegar
- 1/4 cup fresh basil leaves
- 2 Tbsp olive oil
- Salt and pepper to taste

DIRECTIONS:

- Brush eggplant slices with olive oil and season with salt and pepper.
- Preheat grill to medium-high heat and grill eggplant slices for 5 min on each side until tender.
- Layer grilled eggplant and tomato slices on a serving plate, drizzling each layer with balsamic vinegar.
- Garnish with fresh basil leaves before serving.

TIPS:

- Serve as a side dish or light main course.
- Top with feta cheese for added flavor.

N.V.: Calories: 150, Fat: 9g, Carbs: 18g, Protein: 3g, Sugar: 9g

CURRIED CAULIFLOWER RICE BOWL

PREPARATION TIME: 10 min - **COOKING TIME:** 15 min

MODE OF COOKING: Sautéing - **SERVINGS:** 4

INGREDIENTS:

- 1 head cauliflower, grated into rice-sized pieces
- 1 cup frozen peas
- 1/2 cup carrots, diced
- 1 onion, chopped
- 2 cloves garlic, minced
- 1 Tbsp curry powder
- 2 Tbsp coconut oil
- Salt and pepper to taste
- 1/4 cup chopped fresh cilantro

DIRECTIONS:

- Heat coconut oil in a large skillet over medium heat. Sauté onion and garlic until onion is soft.
- Add carrots and cook for 5 min until tender.
- Stir in cauliflower rice, peas, and curry powder. Cook for 5 min, stirring frequently.
- Season with salt and pepper, and garnish with cilantro before serving.

TIPS:

- Pair with grilled chicken for added protein.
- Adjust curry powder for desired spice level.

N.V.: Calories: 140, Fat: 8g, Carbs: 15g, Protein: 3g, Sugar: 5g

SPINACH AND FETA STUFFED PORTOBELLO MUSHROOMS

PREPARATION TIME: 10 min - **COOKING TIME:** 20 min

MODE OF COOKING: Baking - **SERVINGS:** 4

INGREDIENTS:

- 4 large Portobello mushroom caps, stems removed
- 2 cups fresh spinach, chopped
- 1/2 cup feta cheese, crumbled
- 1/4 cup sun-dried tomatoes, chopped
- 2 cloves garlic, minced
- 1 Tbsp olive oil
- Salt and pepper to taste

DIRECTIONS:

- Preheat oven to 375°F (190°C).
- Brush mushroom caps with olive oil and place on a baking sheet.
- In a bowl, combine spinach, feta, sun-dried tomatoes, garlic, salt, and pepper.
- Stuff each mushroom cap with the spinach mixture.
- Bake for 20 min until mushrooms are tender and filling is heated through.

TIPS:

- Serve with a side of quinoa for a complete meal.
- Drizzle with balsamic glaze for extra flavor.

N.V.: Calories: 180, Fat: 12g, Carbs: 10g, Protein: 8g, Sugar: 4g

ROASTED BEET AND ORANGE SALAD

PREPARATION TIME: 15 min - **COOKING TIME:** 45 min

MODE OF COOKING: Roasting - **SERVINGS:** 4

INGREDIENTS:

- 4 medium beets, scrubbed and trimmed
- 2 navel oranges, peeled and segmented
- 1/4 cup walnuts, toasted and chopped
- 2 cups arugula
- 2 Tbsp olive oil
- 1 Tbsp balsamic vinegar
- Salt and pepper to taste

DIRECTIONS:

- Preheat oven to 400°F (204°C).
- Wrap each beet in aluminum foil and place on a baking sheet. Roast for 45 min until tender.
- Once cooled, peel and slice beets.
- In a large bowl, combine beets, orange segments, walnuts, and arugula.
- Whisk together olive oil, balsamic vinegar, salt, and pepper, and drizzle over salad before serving.

TIPS:

- Top with goat cheese for added creaminess.
- Pair with grilled chicken for a heartier meal.

N.V.: Calories: 200, Fat: 12g, Carbs: 23g, Protein: 4g, Sugar: 16g

ZUCCHINI NOODLES WITH PESTO AND CHERRY TOMATOES

PREPARATION TIME: 10 min - **COOKING TIME:** 5 min

MODE OF COOKING: Sautéing - **SERVINGS:** 4

INGREDIENTS:

- 4 medium zucchinis, spiralized
- 1 cup cherry tomatoes, halved

- 1/4 cup pesto sauce
- 1 Tbsp olive oil
- Salt and pepper to taste
- Grated Parmesan cheese for garnish (optional)

DIRECTIONS:

- Heat olive oil in a large skillet over medium heat. Add zucchini noodles and sauté for 2-3 min.
- Add cherry tomatoes and cook for an additional 2 min until slightly softened.
- Remove from heat and toss with pesto sauce, salt, and pepper.
- Garnish with Parmesan cheese before serving.

TIPS:

- Use store-bought pesto for convenience.
- Add grilled shrimp for extra protein.

N.V.: Calories: 180, Fat: 14g, Carbs: 10g, Protein: 4g, Sugar: 4g

Portable and Satisfying Meals for Work or Home

Finding the right balance between convenience and nutrition can be a challenge, especially when juggling the demands of work and home life. However, with a little planning, you can enjoy **portable and satisfying meals** that not only fit into your 1200-calorie plan but also keep you energized throughout the day.

Start by preparing meals that are easy to pack and require minimal reheating. Think of dishes that combine **lean proteins**, healthy fats, and plenty of vegetables. For instance, a grilled chicken salad with mixed greens, cherry tomatoes, and a sprinkle of nuts offers both nutrition and flavor. Dress it with a simple olive oil and lemon vinaigrette for an added zest.

Another great option is a **vegetable stir-fry** with tofu or shrimp. Use a medley of colorful vegetables like bell peppers, broccoli, and snap peas. Season with low-sodium soy sauce and ginger for a satisfying, low-calorie meal. These dishes can be easily stored in airtight containers, ensuring freshness and taste.

Don't forget about snacks! Keep a stash of **healthy snacks** like almonds, apple slices, or carrot sticks within reach. These will help curb hunger between meals and keep your energy levels stable.

By incorporating these strategies, you can maintain your dietary goals and enjoy meals that are both delicious and convenient, no matter where your day takes you.

DINNERS

SPICED LENTIL AND PUMPKIN STEW

PREPARATION TIME: 20 min - **COOKING TIME:** 40 min

MODE OF COOKING: Simmering - **SERVINGS:** 4

INGREDIENTS:

- 1 cup red lentils, rinsed
- 2 cups pumpkin, diced
- 1 onion, finely chopped
- 2 cloves garlic, minced
- 1 tsp cumin seeds
- 1 tsp coriander powder
- 1/2 tsp turmeric powder
- 1/4 tsp cayenne pepper
- 1 Tbsp olive oil
- 4 cups vegetable broth
- Salt and pepper to taste
- Fresh cilantro for garnish

DIRECTIONS:

- In a large pot, heat olive oil over medium heat and sauté onion and garlic until translucent.
- Add cumin seeds, coriander, turmeric, and cayenne pepper, stirring for 1 min until fragrant.
- Stir in pumpkin and lentils, coating them with the spice mixture.
- Pour in vegetable broth, bring to a boil, then reduce heat and simmer for 30 min until lentils are tender.
- Season with salt and pepper, garnish with fresh cilantro before serving.

TIPS:

- Add a squeeze of lime for extra zest.

N.V.: Calories: 220, Fat: 4g, Carbs: 38g, Protein: 12g, Sugar: 6g

HERB-CRUSTED COD WITH LEMON AIOLI

PREPARATION TIME: 15 min - **COOKING TIME:** 20 min

MODE OF COOKING: Baking - **SERVINGS:** 4

INGREDIENTS:

- 4 cod fillets
- 1 cup panko breadcrumbs
- 2 Tbsp parsley, finely chopped
- 1 Tbsp dill, finely chopped
- Zest of 1 lemon
- 2 Tbsp olive oil
- Salt and pepper to taste
- 1/2 cup mayonnaise
- Juice of 1 lemon
- 1 clove garlic, minced

DIRECTIONS:

- Preheat oven to 400°F (204°C).
- Mix panko, parsley, dill, lemon zest, olive oil, salt, and pepper in a bowl.
- Press the crumb mixture onto the top of each cod fillet.
- Place fillets on a baking sheet and bake for 15-20 min until fish is opaque and crust is golden.
- For aioli, combine mayonnaise, lemon juice, and garlic. Serve with baked cod.

TIPS:

- Pair with steamed asparagus for a complete meal.

N.V.: Calories: 320, Fat: 18g, Carbs: 12g, Protein: 28g, Sugar: 1g

QUINOA-STUFFED BELL PEPPERS

PREPARATION TIME: 15 min - **COOKING TIME:** 30 min

MODE OF COOKING: Baking - **SERVINGS:** 4

INGREDIENTS:

- 4 large bell peppers, halved and seeded
- 1 cup quinoa, rinsed
- 2 cups vegetable broth
- 1 can black beans, drained and rinsed
- 1 cup corn kernels
- 1 tsp cumin powder
- 1 tsp smoked paprika
- 1/2 cup feta cheese, crumbled
- Salt and pepper to taste

DIRECTIONS:

- Preheat oven to 375°F (190°C).
- Cook quinoa in vegetable broth according to package instructions.
- Mix cooked quinoa with black beans, corn, cumin, smoked paprika, salt, and pepper.
- Stuff each pepper half with the quinoa mixture and place in a baking dish.
- Bake for 25-30 min until peppers are tender.
- Sprinkle with feta cheese before serving.

TIPS:

- Add chopped cilantro for a fresh finish.

N.V.: Calories: 290, Fat: 8g, Carbs: 45g, Protein: 12g, Sugar: 5g

CHICKPEA AND SPINACH CURRY

PREPARATION TIME: 10 min - **COOKING TIME:** 20 min

MODE OF COOKING: Simmering - **SERVINGS:** 4

INGREDIENTS:

- 1 can chickpeas, drained and rinsed
- 2 cups fresh spinach, chopped
- 1 onion, finely chopped
- 2 cloves garlic, minced
- 1 Tbsp ginger, grated
- 1 tsp garam masala
- 1 tsp curry powder
- 1/2 tsp red chili flakes
- 1 can coconut milk
- 1 Tbsp olive oil
- Salt and pepper to taste

DIRECTIONS:

- Heat olive oil in a large pan over medium heat, sauté onion, garlic, and ginger until fragrant.
- Add garam masala, curry powder, and chili flakes, stirring for 1 min.
- Add chickpeas and coconut milk, bring to a simmer.
- Stir in spinach, cooking until wilted.
- Season with salt and pepper before serving.

TIPS:

- Serve with brown rice for a hearty meal.

N.V.: Calories: 250, Fat: 12g, Carbs: 28g, Protein: 8g, Sugar: 4g

TURMERIC CAULIFLOWER STEAKS

PREPARATION TIME: 10 min - **COOKING TIME:** 30 min

MODE OF COOKING: Roasting - **SERVINGS:** 4

INGREDIENTS:

- 1 large cauliflower, cut into 1-inch steaks
- 2 Tbsp olive oil
- 1 tsp turmeric powder
- 1/2 tsp smoked paprika
- 1/2 tsp garlic powder
- Salt and pepper to taste
- Lemon wedges for serving

DIRECTIONS:

- Preheat oven to 425°F (218°C).
- Mix olive oil, turmeric, smoked paprika, garlic powder, salt, and pepper in a bowl.
- Brush mixture onto both sides of cauliflower steaks.
- Place on a baking sheet and roast for 25-30 min until golden and tender.
- Serve with lemon wedges.

TIPS:

- Top with toasted almonds for a crunchy finish.

N.V.: Calories: 110, Fat: 7g, Carbs: 11g, Protein: 3g, Sugar: 3g

SESAME GINGER TOFU STIR-FRY

PREPARATION TIME: 15 min - **COOKING TIME:** 15 min

MODE OF COOKING: Stir-frying - **SERVINGS:** 4

INGREDIENTS:

- 1 block firm tofu, pressed and cubed
- 2 Tbsp sesame oil
- 1 Tbsp soy sauce
- 1 Tbsp ginger, grated
- 2 cloves garlic, minced
- 1 red bell pepper, sliced
- 1 cup broccoli florets
- 2 Tbsp sesame seeds
- 2 green onions, sliced
- Salt and pepper to taste

DIRECTIONS:

- Heat sesame oil in a large pan over medium-high heat.
- Add tofu cubes, cooking until golden on all sides.
- Add ginger and garlic, sauté for 1 min.
- Stir in bell pepper, broccoli, and soy sauce, cooking until vegetables are tender-crisp.
- Garnish with sesame seeds and green onions before serving.

TIPS:

- Serve over quinoa for added protein.

N.V.: Calories: 220, Fat: 14g, Carbs: 12g, Protein: 14g, Sugar: 3g

MISO GLAZED EGGPLANT

PREPARATION TIME: 10 min - **COOKING TIME:** 25 min

MODE OF COOKING: Broiling - **SERVINGS:** 4

INGREDIENTS:

- 2 large eggplants, halved lengthwise
- 3 Tbsp miso paste
- 2 Tbsp mirin
- 1 Tbsp soy sauce
- 1 Tbsp sesame oil
- 1 Tbsp honey
- 2 green onions, chopped
- 1 Tbsp sesame seeds

DIRECTIONS:

- Preheat broiler to high.
- Score eggplant flesh in a crisscross pattern, be careful not to cut through the skin.
- Mix miso paste, mirin, soy sauce, sesame oil, and honey in a bowl.
- Brush miso mixture over eggplant halves.
- Broil for 20-25 min until eggplants are tender and caramelized.
- Garnish with green onions and sesame seeds before serving.

TIPS:

- Pair with a side of steamed rice.

N.V.: Calories: 180, Fat: 8g, Carbs: 24g, Protein: 4g, Sugar: 10g

ZUCCHINI NOODLES WITH AVOCADO PESTO

PREPARATION TIME: 10 min - **COOKING TIME:** 5 min

MODE OF COOKING: Sautéing - **SERVINGS:** 4

INGREDIENTS:

- 4 medium zucchinis, spiralized
- 2 ripe avocados
- 1 cup fresh basil leaves
- 1/4 cup pine nuts
- 2 cloves garlic
- 2 Tbsp lemon juice
- 2 Tbsp olive oil
- Salt and pepper to taste
- Cherry tomatoes for garnish

DIRECTIONS:

- Blend avocados, basil, pine nuts, garlic, lemon juice, olive oil, salt, and pepper until smooth.
- Heat a non-stick pan over medium heat, add zucchini noodles and sauté for 2-3 min.
- Toss noodles with avocado pesto until well coated.
- Garnish with cherry tomatoes before serving.

TIPS:

- Top with grated parmesan for extra flavor.

N.V.: Calories: 250, Fat: 20g, Carbs: 16g, Protein: 5g, Sugar: 5g

FAMILY-FRIENDLY RECIPES UNDER 300 CALORIES

SPICED CHICKPEA AND KALE SAUTÉ

PREPARATION TIME: 10 min - **COOKING TIME:** 15 min

MODE OF COOKING: Sautéing - **SERVINGS:** 4

INGREDIENTS:

- 1 can (15 oz) chickpeas, drained and rinsed
- 2 cups kale, chopped
- 1 Tbsp olive oil
- 1 tsp cumin seeds
- 1 tsp smoked paprika
- 1/2 tsp turmeric powder
- Salt and pepper to taste
- 1 lemon, juiced
- 2 cloves garlic, minced

DIRECTIONS:

- Heat olive oil in a large skillet over medium heat.
- Add cumin seeds and garlic, sauté for 1 min until fragrant.
- Stir in chickpeas, smoked paprika, turmeric, salt, and pepper. Cook for 5 min.
- Add kale and lemon juice, sauté until kale is wilted, about 5 min.

TIPS:

- Serve with a dollop of Greek yogurt for added creaminess.
- Garnish with fresh cilantro for a burst of flavor.

N.V.: Calories: 180, Fat: 6g, Carbs: 24g, Protein: 7g, Sugar: 2g

HERBED QUINOA AND EDAMAME SALAD

PREPARATION TIME: 15 min - **COOKING TIME:** 15 min

MODE OF COOKING: Boiling - **SERVINGS:** 4

INGREDIENTS:

- 1 cup quinoa
- 1 1/2 cups vegetable broth
- 1 cup shelled edamame
- 1/4 cup fresh parsley, chopped
- 1/4 cup fresh mint, chopped
- 2 Tbsp lemon juice
- 2 Tbsp olive oil
- Salt and pepper to taste

DIRECTIONS:

- Rinse quinoa under cold water.
- In a pot, bring vegetable broth to a boil, add quinoa, reduce heat, cover, and simmer for 15 min.
- In the last 5 min of cooking, add edamame to the pot.
- Fluff quinoa with a fork, stir in parsley, mint, lemon juice, olive oil, salt, and pepper.

TIPS:

- Chill before serving for a refreshing salad option.

N.V.: Calories: 220, Fat: 9g, Carbs: 28g, Protein: 8g, Sugar: 1g

SWEET POTATO AND BLACK BEAN TACOS

PREPARATION TIME: 10 min - **COOKING TIME:** 20 min

MODE OF COOKING: Baking - **SERVINGS:** 4

INGREDIENTS:

- 2 medium sweet potatoes, peeled and diced
- 1 can (15 oz) black beans, drained and rinsed
- 1 Tbsp olive oil

- 1 tsp chili powder
- 1/2 tsp ground cumin
- Salt and pepper to taste
- 8 small corn tortillas
- 1/4 cup red onion, finely chopped
- 1/4 cup cilantro, chopped
- 1 lime, cut into wedges

DIRECTIONS:

- Preheat oven to 400°F (204°C).
- Toss sweet potatoes with olive oil, chili powder, cumin, salt, and pepper.
- Spread on a baking sheet, bake for 20 min, stirring halfway through.
- Warm tortillas, fill with sweet potatoes, black beans, red onion, and cilantro. Serve with lime wedges.

TIPS:

- Add avocado slices for a creamy texture.

N.V.: Calories: 290, Fat: 6g, Carbs: 52g, Protein: 9g, Sugar: 5g

CURRIED CAULIFLOWER SOUP

PREPARATION TIME: 10 min - **COOKING TIME:** 30 min

MODE OF COOKING: Simmering - **SERVINGS:** 4

INGREDIENTS:

- 1 head cauliflower, chopped
- 1 onion, diced
- 2 cloves garlic, minced
- 1 Tbsp olive oil
- 1 Tbsp curry powder

- 4 cups vegetable broth
- 1/2 cup coconut milk
- Salt and pepper to taste

DIRECTIONS:

- In a large pot, heat olive oil over medium heat. Add onion and garlic, sauté for 5 min.
- Add cauliflower and curry powder, stir to coat.
- Pour in vegetable broth, bring to a boil, reduce heat, and simmer for 20 min until cauliflower is tender.
- Blend soup until smooth, stir in coconut milk, season with salt and pepper.

TIPS:

- Garnish with fresh cilantro and a drizzle of coconut milk for presentation.

N.V.: Calories: 150, Fat: 8g, Carbs: 18g, Protein: 4g, Sugar: 5g

GINGER-LIME GRILLED SHRIMP

PREPARATION TIME: 10 min - **COOKING TIME:** 10 min

MODE OF COOKING: Grilling - **SERVINGS:** 4

INGREDIENTS:

- 1 lb shrimp, peeled and deveined
- 2 Tbsp olive oil
- 2 Tbsp lime juice
- 1 Tbsp fresh ginger, grated
- 1 clove garlic, minced
- Salt and pepper to taste
- 1/4 cup fresh cilantro, chopped

DIRECTIONS:

- In a bowl, mix olive oil, lime juice, ginger, garlic, salt, and pepper.

- Add shrimp, toss to coat, and marinate for 10 min.
- Preheat grill to medium-high heat.
- Grill shrimp for 2-3 min on each side until cooked through.
- Garnish with cilantro before serving.

TIPS:

- Serve with a side of quinoa or a green salad.

N.V.: Calories: 200, Fat: 10g, Carbs: 3g, Protein: 24g, Sugar: 0g

ZESTY LEMON HERB CHICKEN

PREPARATION TIME: 10 min - **COOKING TIME:** 25 min

MODE OF COOKING: Baking - **SERVINGS:** 4

INGREDIENTS:

- 4 boneless, skinless chicken breasts
- 2 Tbsp olive oil
- 2 Tbsp lemon juice
- 1 Tbsp fresh rosemary, chopped
- 1 Tbsp fresh thyme, chopped
- Salt and pepper to taste
- 1 lemon, sliced

DIRECTIONS:

- Preheat oven to 375°F (190°C).
- Mix olive oil, lemon juice, rosemary, thyme, salt, and pepper in a bowl.
- Place chicken in a baking dish, pour mixture over, and top with lemon slices.
- Bake for 25 min or until chicken is cooked through.

TIPS:

- Pair with steamed vegetables or a simple salad.

N.V.: Calories: 210, Fat: 9g, Carbs: 1g, Protein: 30g, Sugar: 0g

ROASTED BEET AND FETA SALAD

PREPARATION TIME: 10 min - **COOKING TIME:** 40 min

MODE OF COOKING: Roasting - **SERVINGS:** 4

INGREDIENTS:

- 4 medium beets, peeled and diced
- 2 Tbsp olive oil
- Salt and pepper to taste
- 1/4 cup feta cheese, crumbled
- 1/4 cup walnuts, toasted
- 2 cups arugula
- 2 Tbsp balsamic vinegar

DIRECTIONS:

- Preheat oven to 400°F (204°C).
- Toss beets with olive oil, salt, and pepper.
- Spread on a baking sheet and roast for 40 min until tender.
- In a salad bowl, combine roasted beets, feta, walnuts, and arugula.
- Drizzle with balsamic vinegar before serving.

TIPS:

- For added sweetness, include a handful of dried cranberries.

N.V.: Calories: 250, Fat: 14g, Carbs: 24g, Protein: 7g, Sugar: 13g

EGGPLANT AND LENTIL STEW

PREPARATION TIME: 15 min - **COOKING TIME:** 35 min

MODE OF COOKING: Simmering - **SERVINGS:** 4

INGREDIENTS:

- 1 large eggplant, diced
- 1 cup dried lentils, rinsed
- 1 onion, chopped
- 2 cloves garlic, minced
- 2 Tbsp olive oil
- 1 tsp ground cumin
- 1 tsp ground coriander
- 4 cups vegetable broth
- Salt and pepper to taste

DIRECTIONS:

- Heat olive oil in a large pot over medium heat. Add onion and garlic, sauté for 5 min.
- Stir in eggplant, cumin, coriander, salt, and pepper. Cook for 5 min.
- Add lentils and vegetable broth, bring to a boil, then reduce heat and simmer for 25 min until lentils are tender.

TIPS:

- Garnish with fresh parsley and a squeeze of lemon juice for brightness.

N.V.: Calories: 230, Fat: 9g, Carbs: 30g, Protein: 10g, Sugar: 6g

SNACKS AND DESSERTS

CHIA AND MATCHA ENERGY BITES

PREPARATION TIME: 10 min - **COOKING TIME:** 0 min

MODE OF COOKING: No-cook - **SERVINGS:** 10 bites

INGREDIENTS:

- 1 cup rolled oats
- 2 Tbsp chia seeds
- 1 Tbsp matcha powder
- 1/4 cup almond butter
- 3 Tbsp honey
- 1/4 cup unsweetened coconut flakes
- 1 tsp vanilla extract
- Pinch of salt

DIRECTIONS:

- In a large bowl, combine oats, chia seeds, matcha powder, and salt.
- Add almond butter, honey, and vanilla extract to the dry ingredients. Mix until well combined.
- Fold in coconut flakes.
- Roll mixture into 1-inch balls and refrigerate for 30 minutes before serving.

TIPS:

- Store in an airtight container for up to a week.
- For a nut-free version, substitute sunflower seed butter for almond butter.

N.V.: Calories: 80, Fat: 3.5g, Carbs: 10g, Protein: 2g, Sugar: 5g

SPICY AVOCADO HUMMUS

PREPARATION TIME: 10 min - **COOKING TIME:** 0 min

MODE OF COOKING: No-cook - **SERVINGS:** 4

INGREDIENTS:

- 1 ripe avocado, peeled and pitted
- 1 cup canned chickpeas, drained and rinsed
- 2 Tbsp tahini
- 1 Tbsp lime juice
- 1 clove garlic, minced
- 1/2 tsp cayenne pepper
- Salt and pepper to taste
- 2 Tbsp olive oil

DIRECTIONS:

- In a food processor, combine avocado, chickpeas, tahini, lime juice, garlic, and cayenne pepper.
- Process until smooth, scraping down the sides as needed.
- Season with salt and pepper, then drizzle with olive oil before serving.

TIPS:

- Serve with raw vegetables or whole-grain pita chips.
- Add more cayenne for extra heat.

N.V.: Calories: 150, Fat: 11g, Carbs: 12g, Protein: 3g, Sugar: 1g

Quinoa and Pomegranate Parfait

PREPARATION TIME: 5 min - **COOKING TIME:** 15 min

MODE OF COOKING: Boiling - **SERVINGS:** 2

INGREDIENTS:

- 1/2 cup quinoa, rinsed
- 1 cup water
- 1/2 cup Greek yogurt
- 1/4 cup pomegranate seeds

- 1 Tbsp honey
- 1/4 tsp cinnamon

DIRECTIONS:

- In a saucepan, combine quinoa and water. Bring to a boil, reduce heat, and simmer for 15 minutes or until water is absorbed.
- Let quinoa cool slightly, then layer in a glass with Greek yogurt and pomegranate seeds.
- Drizzle with honey and sprinkle with cinnamon before serving.

TIPS:

- Prepare quinoa in advance and store in the refrigerator for quick assembly.
- Substitute pomegranate with berries for a different flavor.

N.V.: Calories: 180, Fat: 4g, Carbs: 28g, Protein: 8g, Sugar: 14g

ROASTED CHICKPEAS WITH SMOKED PAPRIKA

PREPARATION TIME: 5 min - **COOKING TIME:** 30 min

MODE OF COOKING: Baking - **SERVINGS:** 4

INGREDIENTS:

- 1 can chickpeas, drained and rinsed
- 1 Tbsp olive oil
- 1 tsp smoked paprika
- 1/2 tsp garlic powder
- Salt and pepper to taste

DIRECTIONS:

- Preheat oven to 400°F (204°C).
- Pat chickpeas dry with a paper towel, then toss with olive oil, smoked paprika, garlic powder, salt, and pepper.
- Spread on a baking sheet and roast for 30 minutes, stirring halfway through.

TIPS:

- Ensure chickpeas are dry before roasting for maximum crispiness.

N.V.: Calories: 100, Fat: 3g, Carbs: 15g, Protein: 5g, Sugar: 1g

FROZEN YOGURT BARK WITH BERRIES

PREPARATION TIME: 10 min - **COOKING TIME:** 0 min

MODE OF COOKING: Freezing - **SERVINGS:** 8 pieces

INGREDIENTS:

- 2 cups Greek yogurt
- 1/4 cup honey
- 1/2 cup mixed berries (strawberries, blueberries, raspberries)
- 1/4 cup granola

DIRECTIONS:

- Line a baking sheet with parchment paper.
- Mix Greek yogurt and honey in a bowl, then spread evenly on the prepared baking sheet.
- Sprinkle berries and granola over the yogurt.
- Freeze for at least 4 hours, then break into pieces before serving.

TIPS:

- Use parchment paper to prevent sticking.
- Store in a freezer-safe container for up to 2 weeks.

N.V.: Calories: 120, Fat: 3g, Carbs: 18g, Protein: 6g, Sugar: 11g

SWEET POTATO AND BLACK BEAN MINI TACOS

PREPARATION TIME: 10 min - **COOKING TIME:** 20 min

MODE OF COOKING: Sautéing - **SERVINGS:** 8 mini tacos

INGREDIENTS:

- 1 medium sweet potato, peeled and diced
- 1 Tbsp olive oil
- 1/2 cup canned black beans, drained and rinsed
- 1 tsp cumin
- 1/2 tsp chili powder
- Salt and pepper to taste
- 8 mini corn tortillas
- 1/4 cup chopped cilantro
- 1 lime, cut into wedges

DIRECTIONS:

- Heat olive oil in a skillet over medium heat. Add sweet potato and sauté until tender, about 15 minutes.
- Add black beans, cumin, chili powder, salt, and pepper. Cook for an additional 5 minutes.
- Warm tortillas in a dry skillet, then fill with sweet potato and black bean mixture.
- Garnish with cilantro and serve with lime wedges.

TIPS:

- For added flavor, top with avocado slices or a dollop of Greek yogurt.

N.V.: Calories: 110, Fat: 3g, Carbs: 18g, Protein: 3g, Sugar: 2g

COCONUT AND LIME CHIA PUDDING

PREPARATION TIME: 5 min - **COOKING TIME:** 0 min (chill overnight)

MODE OF COOKING: No-cook - **SERVINGS:** 2

INGREDIENTS:

- 1/4 cup chia seeds
- 1 cup coconut milk
- 1 Tbsp honey

- 1 lime, juiced and zested
- 1/4 cup shredded coconut

DIRECTIONS:

- In a bowl, combine chia seeds, coconut milk, honey, lime juice, and zest.
- Stir well, cover, and refrigerate overnight.
- Before serving, stir again and top with shredded coconut.

TIPS:

- For added texture, top with fresh fruit like mango or pineapple.

N.V.: Calories: 160, Fat: 10g, Carbs: 15g, Protein: 3g, Sugar: 10g

SPICED APPLE AND WALNUT MUFFINS

PREPARATION TIME: 15 min - **COOKING TIME:** 25 min

MODE OF COOKING: Baking - **SERVINGS:** 12 muffins

INGREDIENTS:

- 1 1/2 cups whole wheat flour
- 1/2 cup rolled oats
- 1 tsp baking powder
- 1/2 tsp baking soda
- 1 tsp cinnamon
- 1/4 tsp nutmeg
- 1/2 cup unsweetened applesauce
- 1/4 cup honey
- 1/4 cup olive oil
- 2 eggs
- 1 tsp vanilla extract

- 1 apple, peeled and diced
- 1/4 cup chopped walnuts

DIRECTIONS:

- Preheat oven to 350°F (175°C) and line a muffin tin with paper liners.
- In a bowl, whisk together flour, oats, baking powder, baking soda, cinnamon, and nutmeg.
- In another bowl, mix applesauce, honey, olive oil, eggs, and vanilla extract.
- Combine wet and dry ingredients, then fold in apple and walnuts.
- Divide batter among muffin cups and bake for 25 minutes or until a toothpick comes out clean.

TIPS:

- Store in an airtight container for up to 3 days or freeze for longer storage.

N.V.: Calories: 130, Fat: 5g, Carbs: 19g, Protein: 3g, Sugar: 8g

GUILT-FREE INDULGENCES TO STAY ON TRACK

SPICED CHICKPEA AND QUINOA SALAD

PREPARATION TIME: 10 min - **COOKING TIME:** 20 min

MODE OF COOKING: Boiling - **SERVINGS:** 4

INGREDIENTS:

- 1 cup quinoa, rinsed
- 2 cups water
- 1 can (15 oz.) chickpeas, drained and rinsed
- 1 red bell pepper, diced
- 1 cucumber, diced
- 1/4 cup chopped fresh parsley
- 1 tsp ground cumin
- 1 tsp smoked paprika

- 2 Tbsp lemon juice
- 1 Tbsp olive oil
- Salt and pepper to taste

DIRECTIONS:

- In a saucepan, bring quinoa and water to a boil. Reduce heat, cover, and simmer for 15 min or until water is absorbed.
- Fluff quinoa with a fork, then let it cool slightly.
- In a large bowl, combine chickpeas, bell pepper, cucumber, and parsley.
- In a small bowl, whisk together cumin, paprika, lemon juice, olive oil, salt, and pepper.
- Add quinoa to the vegetable mixture and drizzle with dressing. Toss to combine.

TIPS:

- Serve chilled for a refreshing taste.
- Add feta cheese for extra flavor.

N.V.: Calories: 210, Fat: 6g, Carbs: 34g, Protein: 8g, Sugar: 3g

HERBED CAULIFLOWER RICE WITH ALMONDS

PREPARATION TIME: 10 min - **COOKING TIME:** 10 min

MODE OF COOKING: Sautéing - **SERVINGS:** 4

INGREDIENTS:

- 1 medium cauliflower, grated
- 2 Tbsp olive oil
- 1/4 cup sliced almonds
- 2 cloves garlic, minced
- 1/4 cup chopped fresh cilantro
- 1 Tbsp lemon zest
- Salt and pepper to taste

DIRECTIONS:

- Heat olive oil in a large skillet over medium heat.
- Add almonds and sauté until golden brown, about 2 min.
- Add garlic and cook for 1 min until fragrant.
- Stir in grated cauliflower, cooking for 5 min until tender.
- Remove from heat and mix in cilantro, lemon zest, salt, and pepper.

TIPS:

- Use a food processor to grate cauliflower quickly.
- Pair with grilled chicken for a complete meal.

N.V.: Calories: 120, Fat: 8g, Carbs: 10g, Protein: 4g, Sugar: 3g

ROASTED RED PEPPER HUMMUS

PREPARATION TIME: 10 min - **COOKING TIME:** 0 min

MODE OF COOKING: Blending - **SERVINGS:** 6

INGREDIENTS:

- 1 can (15 oz.) chickpeas, drained and rinsed
- 1/2 cup roasted red peppers
- 1/4 cup tahini
- 2 Tbsp lemon juice
- 2 cloves garlic
- 1 Tbsp olive oil
- 1 tsp ground cumin
- Salt and pepper to taste

DIRECTIONS:

- In a food processor, combine chickpeas, red peppers, tahini, lemon juice, garlic, and olive oil.

- Blend until smooth, adding water as needed for desired consistency.
- Season with cumin, salt, and pepper, blend again.

TIPS:

- Serve with sliced vegetables for a healthy snack.
- Store in the fridge for up to a week.

N.V.: Calories: 140, Fat: 6g, Carbs: 18g, Protein: 5g, Sugar: 2g

EGGPLANT CAPONATA

PREPARATION TIME: 15 min - **COOKING TIME:** 30 min

MODE OF COOKING: Simmering - **SERVINGS:** 4

INGREDIENTS:

- 1 large eggplant, diced
- 1 onion, chopped
- 2 cloves garlic, minced
- 2 Tbsp olive oil
- 1 can (14 oz.) diced tomatoes
- 1/4 cup chopped green olives
- 2 Tbsp capers
- 1 Tbsp red wine vinegar
- 1 Tbsp sugar
- Salt and pepper to taste

DIRECTIONS:

- Heat olive oil in a large pan over medium heat.
- Add eggplant and onion, sauté until soft, about 10 min.
- Stir in garlic, tomatoes, olives, capers, vinegar, and sugar.

- Simmer for 20 min, stirring occasionally, until thickened.
- Season with salt and pepper before serving.

TIPS:

- Serve as a topping for grilled meats or fish.
- Can be enjoyed warm or cold.

N.V.: Calories: 110, Fat: 7g, Carbs: 12g, Protein: 2g, Sugar: 5g

ZUCCHINI NOODLES WITH AVOCADO PESTO

PREPARATION TIME: 10 min - **COOKING TIME:** 5 min

MODE OF COOKING: Sautéing - **SERVINGS:** 2

INGREDIENTS:

- 2 medium zucchinis, spiralized
- 1 avocado, peeled and pitted
- 1/4 cup fresh basil leaves
- 2 Tbsp pine nuts
- 1 clove garlic
- 2 Tbsp lemon juice
- 1 Tbsp olive oil
- Salt and pepper to taste

DIRECTIONS:

- In a blender, combine avocado, basil, pine nuts, garlic, lemon juice, and olive oil. Blend until smooth.
- Season pesto with salt and pepper.
- In a skillet, sauté zucchini noodles over medium heat for 2-3 min until slightly softened.

- Toss noodles with avocado pesto and serve immediately.

TIPS:

- Top with cherry tomatoes for added color and flavor.

N.V.: Calories: 250, Fat: 22g, Carbs: 14g, Protein: 4g, Sugar: 4g

SWEET POTATO AND BLACK BEAN TACOS

PREPARATION TIME: 10 min - **COOKING TIME:** 20 min

MODE OF COOKING: Roasting - **SERVINGS:** 4

INGREDIENTS:

- 2 medium sweet potatoes, peeled and cubed
- 1 Tbsp olive oil
- 1 tsp chili powder
- 1 can (15 oz.) black beans, drained and rinsed
- 8 corn tortillas
- 1/4 cup chopped cilantro
- 1 lime, cut into wedges
- Salt and pepper to taste

DIRECTIONS:

- Preheat oven to 400°F (204°C).
- Toss sweet potatoes with olive oil, chili powder, salt, and pepper.
- Spread on a baking sheet and roast for 20 min until tender.
- Warm tortillas in a skillet over medium heat.
- Fill tortillas with roasted sweet potatoes, black beans, and cilantro. Serve with lime wedges.

TIPS:

- Add avocado slices for extra creaminess.

N.V.: Calories: 300, Fat: 6g, Carbs: 54g, Protein: 9g, Sugar: 7g

BAKED FALAFEL WITH TAHINI SAUCE

PREPARATION TIME: 15 min - **COOKING TIME:** 25 min

MODE OF COOKING: Baking - **SERVINGS:** 4

INGREDIENTS:

- 1 can (15 oz.) chickpeas, drained and rinsed
- 1/4 cup chopped parsley
- 2 cloves garlic
- 1 tsp ground cumin
- 1 tsp ground coriander
- 2 Tbsp flour
- Salt and pepper to taste
- 2 Tbsp olive oil
- 1/4 cup tahini
- 2 Tbsp lemon juice
- 2 Tbsp water

DIRECTIONS:

- Preheat oven to 375°F (190°C).
- In a food processor, combine chickpeas, parsley, garlic, cumin, coriander, flour, salt, and pepper. Blend until smooth.
- Form mixture into small patties and place on a baking sheet.
- Brush patties with olive oil and bake for 25 min until golden brown.
- For tahini sauce, whisk together tahini, lemon juice, and water until smooth.
- Serve falafel with tahini sauce.

TIPS:

- Serve in pita bread with fresh veggies.

N.V.: Calories: 270, Fat: 14g, Carbs: 30g, Protein: 8g, Sugar: 1g

PUMPKIN AND LENTIL CURRY

PREPARATION TIME: 10 min - **COOKING TIME:** 30 min

MODE OF COOKING: Simmering - **SERVINGS:** 4

INGREDIENTS:

- 1 Tbsp coconut oil
- 1 onion, chopped
- 2 cloves garlic, minced
- 1 Tbsp grated ginger
- 1 tsp turmeric
- 1 tsp ground cumin
- 1 can (15 oz.) pumpkin puree
- 1 cup red lentils
- 4 cups vegetable broth
- 1/2 cup coconut milk
- Salt and pepper to taste

DIRECTIONS:

- In a large pot, heat coconut oil over medium heat.
- Add onion, garlic, and ginger, sauté until translucent.
- Stir in turmeric and cumin, cooking for 1 min.
- Add pumpkin puree, lentils, and broth. Bring to a boil, then reduce heat and simmer for 25 min.
- Stir in coconut milk, season with salt and pepper.

TIPS:

- Garnish with fresh cilantro before serving.

N.V.: Calories: 220, Fat: 8g, Carbs: 30g, Protein: 9g, Sugar: 4g

CHAPTER 5: PRACTICAL TIPS FOR SUCCESS

As you embark on this transformative journey, imagine yourself as the hero in your own story. Every step you take towards healthier living is a chapter filled with **determination**, **resilience**, and **growth**. Picture the feeling of waking up each morning with **renewed energy** and a sense of accomplishment, knowing that you are taking control of your life.

One of the most profound realizations you'll encounter is the power of **mindful eating**. In our fast-paced world, it's easy to eat without thinking, letting stress or habit dictate our choices. But when you pause, truly savoring each bite, you begin to understand your body's signals and needs. This awareness fosters a deeper connection with food, transforming meals from mere sustenance into moments of **nourishment** and **gratitude**.

Consider the support of a trusted ally—whether a friend, family member, or even a community group. These connections can be invaluable, offering encouragement and accountability. Sharing your goals and progress with others not only reinforces your commitment but also invites a shared celebration of your victories, no matter how small.

Remember, the path to success is not a solitary one. Embrace the journey with **openness** and a willingness to learn from each experience. Each challenge is an opportunity to grow stronger, more resilient, and ultimately, more aligned with the healthier, happier version of yourself that you are becoming.

PORTION CONTROL AND SERVING SIZES

Understanding **portion control** is a cornerstone of the 1200-calorie diet plan. It's not just about what you eat, but how much you consume. The concept of portion control can sometimes feel overwhelming, especially when faced with a plate full of tempting foods. However, mastering this skill can significantly impact your weight loss journey.

Firstly, it's essential to recognize the difference between a **serving size** and a portion. A serving size is a standard measurement of food, often found on nutrition labels, while a portion is the amount you choose to eat. Many of us are accustomed to larger portions, which can lead to consuming more calories than intended. By adjusting our portions to align with recommended serving sizes, we can effectively manage our calorie intake.

One practical strategy is to use smaller plates and bowls. This simple switch can create the illusion of a fuller plate, helping you feel satisfied with less food. Additionally, be mindful of your hunger cues. Eating slowly and savoring each bite allows your body to signal when it's full, preventing overeating.

Another helpful tip is to **pre-portion snacks** into individual servings. This prevents mindless snacking from large bags or containers, which can quickly add up in calories. Remember, it's not about deprivation but about making conscious choices that align with your goals.

Embrace the power of portion control as a tool to not only manage your weight but also to enhance your overall well-being. With practice, it becomes second nature, empowering you to enjoy your meals while staying committed to your health objectives.

HOW TO MEASURE PORTIONS WITHOUT STRESS

Measuring portions can often feel like a daunting task, especially when you're trying to adhere to a **1200-calorie diet**. But rest assured, it doesn't have to be stressful or complicated. The key is to find methods that fit seamlessly into your daily routine, making portion control a natural part of your lifestyle.

First, let's talk about using your **hand as a measuring tool**. It's always with you, and it's surprisingly effective. For instance, a serving of protein like chicken or fish should be about the size of your palm. Vegetables can fill up your entire fist, while a serving of carbs, such as rice or pasta, is roughly the size of your cupped hand. Fats, like butter or cheese, should be limited to the size of your thumb.

Another helpful tip is to use **smaller plates and bowls**. This simple switch can trick your brain into feeling satisfied with less food. A full small plate often feels more satisfying than a partially filled large one. This visual cue can help you maintain control over your portions without feeling deprived.

Lastly, always take a moment to **pause and assess** your hunger before going back for seconds. Ask yourself if you're truly hungry or if you're eating out of habit or emotion. This mindful approach not only helps with portion control but also encourages a healthier relationship with food.

MANAGING CR INDULGENCES TO STAY ON TRACKAVINGS AND EMOTIONAL EATING

Cravings can feel like a relentless tide, pulling you away from your goals. But understanding their roots can help you regain control. Often, these cravings are not just about hunger; they're tied to **emotions** or **stress**. Recognizing this is the first step in managing them.

When a craving strikes, pause and ask yourself: **What am I truly feeling?** Are you bored, anxious, or perhaps seeking comfort? By identifying the underlying emotion, you can address it more effectively. Instead of reaching for food, consider alternatives like a brisk walk, a few minutes of meditation, or calling a friend.

Another strategy is to **plan indulgences** mindfully. Allow yourself a small treat once in a while, but do so with intention. When you know a treat is coming, it becomes less about impulse and more about enjoyment. This approach helps you maintain balance without feeling deprived.

It's also crucial to keep your environment supportive. Stock your kitchen with **healthy snacks** that satisfy. Fresh fruits, nuts, or yogurt can be both nourishing and fulfilling. By having these options readily available, you're more likely to make choices that align with your goals.

Remember, overcoming cravings is a journey. Each time you choose to address them with awareness, you're building resilience and paving the way for lasting change.

STRATEGIES TO STAY IN CONTROL

Embarking on a 1200-calorie diet plan can feel daunting, but with the right strategies, you can stay in control and make this journey both rewarding and sustainable. One of the first steps is to **set realistic goals**. Understand that weight loss is a gradual process, and setting achievable milestones will help you stay motivated.

It's crucial to **plan your meals ahead**. Taking time to prepare a weekly menu not only saves you from last-minute unhealthy choices but also ensures that you're meeting your nutritional needs. Batch cooking can be a lifesaver, providing you with ready-to-eat meals that keep you on track.

Another key strategy is to **practice mindful eating**. Pay attention to your hunger cues and savor each bite. This approach helps prevent overeating and enhances your appreciation of food. Additionally, staying hydrated is essential. Often, we confuse thirst with hunger, so keeping a water bottle handy can help you distinguish between the two.

Don't underestimate the power of a **support system**. Whether it's friends, family, or online communities, having people who understand your journey can offer encouragement and accountability. Lastly, be kind to yourself. If you have a setback, remember that it's part of the process. Learn from it and move forward with renewed determination.

STAYING MOTIVATED

Embarking on a weight loss journey can feel like climbing a mountain, but remember, it's not about reaching the summit in one leap. It's about taking **consistent, small steps** that lead to big changes. To stay motivated, start by setting **realistic goals**. Break down your ultimate objective into smaller milestones, celebrating each one as a victory. This approach not only makes the journey manageable but also boosts your confidence as you progress.

Surround yourself with a **supportive community**. Whether it's friends, family, or an online group, having people who understand your challenges can make a world of difference. Share your struggles and triumphs, and draw strength from their encouragement.

Remember, motivation is fueled by **purpose**. Reflect on why you started this journey. Whether it's to improve your health, increase your energy, or simply feel better about yourself, keeping your reasons at the forefront will guide you through tough days.

Lastly, be kind to yourself. Setbacks are part of the process, not the end. Use them as learning opportunities, not reasons to give up. Embrace the journey with patience and perseverance, knowing that each day brings you closer to a healthier, more vibrant you.

OVERCOMING SETBACKS AND PLATEAUS

Facing a setback or plateau can feel like a daunting roadblock on your journey to better health. It's essential to remember that these moments are **natural** and even expected. They don't define your success; instead, they offer an opportunity to **learn** and **adapt**.

First, let's address the emotional aspect. It's easy to feel discouraged when progress stalls, but this is the time to practice **self-compassion**. Acknowledge your feelings without judgment. Reflect on your journey so far and celebrate the **milestones** you've already achieved. This shift in perspective can reignite your motivation.

Next, consider the practical side. Re-evaluate your current plan. Are you following your 1200-calorie diet accurately? It's possible that **small deviations** have crept in. Keeping a detailed food diary can help identify areas for adjustment. Additionally, consider varying your **exercise routine** to challenge your body in new ways, potentially breaking through the plateau.

Sometimes, our bodies simply need **time** to adjust to new routines. Patience is your ally. Continue to focus on healthy habits, knowing that persistence will pay off. Remember, each step you take is a step towards a healthier, more vibrant you. Embrace the journey, setbacks and all, with an open heart and a determined spirit.

DINING OUT AND SOCIAL SITUATIONS

Eating out can be a delightful experience, but it often poses challenges when you're committed to a **1200-calorie diet**. With a little planning and a positive mindset, you can enjoy your time without compromising your goals. Here's how:

First, **research the menu** before you go. Most restaurants post their menus online, giving you the chance to choose options that align with your dietary needs. Look for dishes that feature **grilled, baked, or steamed** proteins and ask for sauces or dressings on the side to control your calorie intake.

When ordering, don't hesitate to **customize your meal**. Restaurants are often willing to accommodate requests like swapping fries for a side salad or asking for vegetables instead of rice. These small changes can make a big difference.

Portion control is essential. Consider sharing a dish with a friend or asking for a **to-go box** right away, so you can set aside half of your meal for later. This helps you stay within your calorie limit while still enjoying the dining experience.

In social settings, communicate your goals to those around you. Friends and family are more supportive when they understand your commitment to **health and wellness**. Suggest activities that don't revolve solely around food, like going for a walk or attending a local event.

Remember, the journey to better health is about balance. Enjoy your meals, cherish your company, and know that with each mindful choice, you're stepping closer to the healthier life you envision.

How to Navigate Menus and Stay Compliant

Dining out while adhering to a 1200-calorie diet can feel daunting, but with a few strategic approaches, you can enjoy meals without straying from your plan. The key is to be **mindful** and **prepared**. Start by researching the restaurant's menu online if possible. This allows you to plan your meal choices ahead of time, helping you avoid impulse decisions that might derail your efforts.

When you're at the restaurant, don't hesitate to ask the server about preparation methods or request modifications. Most establishments are accommodating; for instance, you can ask for grilled instead of fried, or request dressings and sauces on the side. This empowers you to control your calorie intake without compromising on taste.

Portion control is another crucial aspect. Consider asking for a half portion or sharing a dish with a friend. Alternatively, you can request a to-go box at the start of the meal and save half for later. This not only helps with calorie management but also extends the enjoyment of dining out.

Finally, remember to stay **hydrated** with water or unsweetened beverages. Often, we confuse thirst with hunger, leading to unnecessary calorie consumption. By maintaining these strategies, you can navigate menus confidently and stay compliant with your dietary goals, all while enjoying the social aspects of dining out.

CHAPTER 6: ADAPTING THE PLAN FOR YOUR NEEDS

Imagine standing at the crossroads of your health journey, where the path to a healthier you is paved with **choices** tailored to your unique needs. This chapter is your guide to adapting the 1200-calorie plan to fit seamlessly into your life, ensuring it's not just a temporary fix but a sustainable lifestyle change.

Picture Sarah, a busy mother of two, who once felt overwhelmed by the idea of maintaining a diet amidst her hectic schedule. She discovered that by **incorporating small, manageable changes** into her daily routine, she could align the diet with her family's meals. Simple swaps, like replacing white rice with quinoa, allowed her to stay on track while sharing meals with her loved ones.

For Mark, a young professional constantly on the go, the challenge was finding time to prepare meals. He learned the value of **meal prepping** on Sundays, turning it into a family activity. This not only saved time but also ensured he always had healthy options at hand, reducing the temptation to opt for quick, unhealthy snacks.

Adaptation is about understanding your **personal triggers** and finding ways to navigate them. Whether it's emotional eating or social pressures, recognizing these challenges is the first step. Remember, this journey is yours. Embrace the flexibility of the plan, and let it evolve with you, guiding you toward a healthier, more fulfilling life.

SPECIAL DIETARY CONSIDERATIONS

When embarking on a journey with the 1200-calorie diet plan, it's crucial to consider any **special dietary needs** you may have. Whether you're dealing with **allergies, intolerances, or specific health conditions**, adapting the plan to fit your personal requirements will ensure a safer and more effective experience.

For those with **food allergies**, it's essential to identify and avoid any triggers. Substitute ingredients that align with your dietary restrictions while maintaining nutritional balance. For example, if you're allergic to nuts, consider using seeds or seed-based products for healthy fats and protein.

If you have **lactose intolerance**, opt for lactose-free dairy products or plant-based alternatives. These can offer similar nutritional benefits without discomfort. Remember, the goal is to find **suitable replacements** that keep you on track without compromising taste or nutrition.

Individuals managing conditions like **diabetes** should prioritize foods that help maintain stable blood sugar levels. Focus on **complex carbohydrates** and fiber-rich foods, which can provide sustained energy and prevent spikes in glucose levels.

For those following a **vegetarian or vegan diet**, ensure you're meeting your protein needs with plant-based sources such as legumes, tofu, and quinoa. These options can seamlessly integrate into your 1200-calorie plan while supporting your dietary preferences.

Ultimately, the key is to approach the diet with **flexibility and awareness**, making adjustments that honor your unique needs. This personalized approach not only enhances your experience but also fosters a sustainable and enjoyable path to better health.

ADJUSTING FOR ALLERGIES, VEGETARIAN OPTIONS, AND MORE

When embarking on a journey to reclaim your health through the 1200-calorie diet plan, it's essential to consider **individual dietary needs** and preferences. Whether you're dealing with **food allergies** or choosing a vegetarian lifestyle, the plan can be adapted to suit your requirements without compromising on nutrition or flavor.

For those with **allergies**, the key is to identify safe substitutes that maintain the nutritional balance of your meals. If you're allergic to nuts, consider seeds like sunflower or pumpkin as alternatives. For dairy allergies, opt for fortified plant-based milks and yogurts to ensure you're still getting essential nutrients like calcium and vitamin D.

Vegetarians can thrive on this plan by incorporating a variety of **plant-based proteins** such as beans, lentils, and tofu. These ingredients not only provide the necessary protein but also add fiber and other vital nutrients to your diet. Experiment with spices and herbs to enhance flavors and keep your meals exciting.

Remember, the goal is to create a diet that is both **satisfying and sustainable**. By being mindful of your unique needs and making thoughtful adjustments, you can fully embrace the 1200-calorie plan and move confidently towards a healthier, more energized life.

Cultural and Personal Preferences

Understanding and respecting **cultural and personal preferences** can significantly impact the success of any dietary plan, including the 1200-calorie diet. Everyone's relationship with food is deeply rooted in their cultural background, traditions, and personal experiences. These elements not only shape what we eat but also how we perceive food and its role in our lives.

For many, food is more than just sustenance; it's a way to connect with family and community. In some cultures, meals are a communal activity, filled with rich flavors and shared experiences. Recognizing this, it's important to adapt the 1200-calorie diet in a way that respects these traditions while still achieving your health goals. This might mean finding creative ways to incorporate traditional ingredients or reimagining beloved recipes in a healthier form.

Personal preferences also play a crucial role. Some people might find comfort in certain foods due to their upbringing or personal tastes. It's essential to find a balance that satisfies your palate without compromising the diet's effectiveness. Experiment with different spices, cooking methods, and ingredient substitutions to maintain the essence of your favorite dishes.

Ultimately, the key is to create a plan that feels **authentic** to you. By honoring your cultural and personal preferences, you're more likely to stick with the diet and enjoy the journey towards better health. Remember, this is not just about losing weight; it's about embracing a lifestyle that reflects who you are while fostering a healthier you.

Substitutions for Common Ingredients

In the journey towards a healthier lifestyle, finding the right **substitutes** for common ingredients can be a game-changer. Imagine savoring your favorite dishes without the guilt, simply by making a few smart swaps. Let's explore some of these transformations that can make your meals both delicious and diet-friendly.

First, consider replacing butter with **avocado** or **applesauce**. These substitutes not only reduce calories but also infuse your dishes with nutrients. Avocado provides healthy fats, while applesauce adds a hint of sweetness without the added sugar.

For those who love pasta, try swapping traditional noodles with **zucchini noodles** or **spaghetti squash**. These alternatives are not only lower in calories but also pack a punch of vitamins and minerals, keeping your meals light and nutritious.

If you're a fan of rice, consider using **cauliflower rice**. This low-carb substitute is easy to make and can be flavored to suit any dish, providing a satisfying and healthy alternative to regular rice.

For baking enthusiasts, using **almond flour** or **coconut flour** instead of regular flour can significantly lower the carb content of your baked goods, while adding a unique flavor and texture.

Remember, these substitutions are not just about cutting calories; they're about **enhancing** your meals with flavors and nutrients that support your health goals. With each swap, you're taking a step towards a more vibrant, energized life.

CHAPTER 7: MOVING BEYOND THE PLATE

As we venture beyond the confines of the dining table, it's crucial to explore the **holistic aspects** of our journey. Weight loss is not just about the calories we consume; it's a **comprehensive lifestyle transformation** that touches every part of our existence. Imagine, for a moment, the ripple effect of each decision you make. Choosing to walk to the store instead of driving not only burns calories but also clears your mind, offering a moment of reflection and peace.

Consider the role of **emotional well-being** in your diet plan. Many of us turn to food for comfort, a temporary solace from stress or anxiety. Yet, by identifying these triggers, we can find healthier outlets. Perhaps it's the simple act of journaling, capturing your thoughts and feelings on paper, or maybe it's a few minutes of meditation, allowing your mind to find stillness amidst the chaos.

Moreover, your journey is not a solitary one. Engage your family and friends, invite them to join you in activities that promote health and connection. A weekend hike or a shared cooking session can transform your social life into a **supportive network**, reinforcing your commitment to change.

Ultimately, moving beyond the plate means embracing a **balanced lifestyle**, where every choice nourishes not only the body but also the spirit. This is your path to a more vibrant, fulfilling life.

THE ROLE OF EXERCISE

Exercise is not just a tool for weight loss; it's a **key component** in transforming your overall well-being. By incorporating regular physical activity into your routine, you're not only burning calories but also boosting your mood, improving sleep, and enhancing your energy levels. The beauty of exercise lies in its versatility—it can be tailored to fit your lifestyle and preferences, making it an enjoyable part of your daily life.

Starting an exercise regimen might seem daunting, especially if you're new to it. The trick is to **start small** and gradually increase your activity level. Begin with activities you enjoy, whether it's walking, dancing, or cycling. The goal is to find something that doesn't feel like a chore but rather a rewarding break in your day.

Consistency is more important than intensity. Aim for at least **30 minutes** of moderate exercise most days of the week. This doesn't have to be continuous; you can break it down into shorter sessions if needed. Remember, every step counts towards your health goals.

Exercise also plays a crucial role in managing stress and emotional eating. When you engage in physical activity, your body releases endorphins—natural mood lifters that can help curb cravings and reduce reliance on food for comfort. This makes exercise a powerful ally in your journey towards a healthier lifestyle.

Finally, don't underestimate the power of social support. Involve friends or family members in your activities, turning exercise into a **social occasion** that strengthens bonds and keeps you motivated. Together, you can celebrate small victories and encourage each other to stay committed to your goals.

WHY PHYSICAL ACTIVITY ENHANCES WEIGHT LOSS

As we embark on this journey to better health, it's crucial to understand the role of **physical activity** in enhancing weight loss. While diet lays the foundation, incorporating movement amplifies the benefits, creating a synergy that accelerates progress. Think of physical activity as a catalyst—it doesn't just burn calories; it transforms the way your body functions.

Engaging in regular exercise boosts your **metabolism**, helping your body become more efficient at using energy. This means that even when you're at rest, your body is working harder to burn calories. Additionally, exercise aids in preserving **lean muscle mass**, which is essential for maintaining a healthy metabolism. The more muscle you have, the more calories you burn, even when you're not actively moving.

Beyond the physical benefits, exercise plays a pivotal role in **emotional well-being**. It releases endorphins, the body's natural mood elevators, which can help alleviate stress and combat the emotional challenges often associated with weight loss. By incorporating physical activity into your routine, you're not only enhancing your physical health but also nurturing your mental resilience.

Remember, the goal isn't to become an athlete overnight. Start with activities you enjoy, whether it's walking, dancing, or swimming. The key is to stay **consistent** and make movement a part of your daily life. As you progress, you'll find that physical activity becomes a source of joy and empowerment, propelling you closer to your weight loss goals.

BEGINNER-FRIENDLY EXERCISES FOR LIMITED MOBILITY

Embarking on a weight loss journey with limited mobility can feel daunting, but it's entirely possible with the right approach. Let's focus on exercises that are both **gentle** and **effective**, ensuring you feel **empowered** every step of the way.

First, consider **chair exercises**. These are perfect for those who require additional support. Start with simple arm raises. Sit up straight, extend your arms to your sides, and slowly lift them above your head. This exercise not only strengthens your upper body but also enhances your **flexibility**.

Next, try **seated leg lifts**. While sitting, extend one leg straight out in front of you, hold for a few seconds, then lower it back down. This movement helps in building leg strength and improving circulation. Remember, consistency is key, so aim for a few repetitions each day.

For those who can stand with support, **wall push-ups** are an excellent option. Stand a few feet away from a wall, place your hands on it at shoulder height, and gently push your body towards the wall and back. This exercise is great for strengthening your arms and chest while being easy on the joints.

Finally, don't underestimate the power of **deep breathing**. It might seem simple, but deep breathing exercises can reduce stress, improve lung capacity, and enhance overall well-being. Take a few minutes each day to focus on your breath, inhaling deeply through your nose and exhaling slowly through your mouth.

Remember, every small step you take is a step towards a healthier, more **vibrant** you. Celebrate your progress, no matter how minor it may seem, and stay committed to your goals. You're not alone on this journey, and with patience and perseverance, you will achieve the change you seek.

MINDSET AND MENTAL HEALTH

Embarking on a journey towards weight loss is as much a mental game as it is a physical one. Our mindset plays a **crucial role** in determining our success. To truly transform our bodies, we must first transform our thoughts.

One of the most powerful tools in your arsenal is the ability to **visualize success**. Picture yourself achieving your goals, feeling healthier, and living a more vibrant life. This mental imagery sets a positive tone and strengthens your resolve.

It's also important to **embrace self-compassion**. On this path, setbacks are natural, but they don't define your journey. Instead of viewing them as failures, see them as opportunities to learn and grow. Treat yourself with the same kindness you would offer a friend.

Another key aspect is **managing stress**. Stress can often lead to emotional eating, which derails progress. Incorporate stress-relief techniques such as meditation, deep breathing, or gentle exercise into your daily routine to maintain emotional balance.

Lastly, surround yourself with a **supportive community**. Share your goals and challenges with friends, family, or support groups who understand and encourage your efforts. Their encouragement can be a powerful motivator and remind you that you're not alone in this journey.

BUILDING CONFIDENCE AND OVERCOMING SELF-DOUBT

Embarking on a weight loss journey is as much a mental challenge as it is a physical one. It's easy to feel overwhelmed by self-doubt, especially when faced with the daunting task of changing long-standing habits. However, building confidence is key to overcoming these hurdles and achieving your goals.

First, recognize that **self-doubt is a natural part of the process**. Everyone experiences moments of uncertainty, but it's how you respond to these feelings that matters. Instead of allowing doubt to derail your progress, use it as a reminder of your strength and commitment. Each step you take, no matter how small, is a victory worth celebrating.

Next, focus on setting **realistic and achievable goals**. Break down your weight loss journey into manageable milestones. This approach not only makes the process less intimidating but also provides regular opportunities for success, boosting your confidence along the way.

Surround yourself with a **supportive community**. Whether it's family, friends, or an online group, having people who understand your journey can offer encouragement and accountability. Share your achievements and challenges with them, and don't hesitate to seek advice when needed.

Finally, practice **self-compassion**. Be kind to yourself, especially on tough days. Remember that setbacks are not failures; they are learning opportunities. Embrace your journey with patience and positivity, and you'll find that confidence grows naturally over time.

CHAPTER 8: SAMPLE 30-DAY MEAL PLAN

As you embark on this transformative journey, imagine each day as a new canvas, ready to be painted with vibrant, nutritious choices. Picture the morning sun casting a warm glow as you prepare a simple yet satisfying breakfast. Perhaps it's a bowl of **oatmeal**, sprinkled with **fresh berries** and a hint of cinnamon, setting a wholesome tone for the day.

Midday arrives, and with it, a chance to recharge. Visualize a colorful salad, brimming with crisp greens, bright cherry tomatoes, and a sprinkle of feta cheese. The tangy vinaigrette dances on your taste buds, a reminder that healthy eating can be both **delicious** and fulfilling.

As the afternoon unfolds, let a small snack of crunchy almonds or a juicy apple be your companion, providing the energy you need to stay focused and engaged. This is not just about sustenance; it's about nurturing your body with intention and care.

Evening descends, and with it, the comforting aroma of a home-cooked meal wafts through your kitchen. Imagine savoring a tender piece of grilled chicken, accompanied by roasted vegetables that glisten with olive oil and herbs. Each bite is a celebration of your commitment to health and well-being.

Throughout these 30 days, let each meal be a moment of **mindful appreciation**, a step towards reclaiming your vitality and confidence. Embrace this journey with an open heart and a curious palate, knowing that every choice you make is a stride towards a healthier, more fulfilling life.

WEEK-BY-WEEK BREAKDOWN

Embarking on this 30-day journey is like setting sail on a path to a healthier, more vibrant you. Each week, we'll tackle new challenges and celebrate victories, big and small. Let's dive into the first week, where the foundation for transformation begins.

In **Week One**, our focus is on understanding and embracing the 1200-calorie framework. This is your chance to familiarize yourself with portion sizes and the types of foods that will fuel your body efficiently. Start by planning your meals with whole foods—think fresh vegetables, lean proteins, and whole grains. It's also important to keep a food diary, noting how different foods make you feel. This awareness will help you make informed choices as you progress.

Moving into **Week Two**, we'll emphasize consistency. By now, you should have a rhythm with your meals, and it's time to introduce light physical activity into your routine. Whether it's a brisk walk or a gentle yoga session, find something you enjoy. Remember, this isn't about punishing your body but rather celebrating its capabilities. Consistency is key, so aim for activity that you can sustain.

As we reach **Week Three**, the focus shifts to overcoming emotional eating. It's natural to turn to food for comfort, but this week, we'll explore alternative coping mechanisms. Consider journaling, meditating, or even picking up a new hobby. Identify your triggers and plan ahead—having a strategy in place will empower you to make healthier choices.

Finally, in **Week Four**, we'll consolidate your new habits. Reflect on your journey and the changes you've noticed in your energy levels and mood. This is also a time to adjust your plan to better fit your lifestyle. Remember, this isn't just a diet; it's a foundation for lifelong health. Celebrate your progress, no matter how small, and look forward to the new possibilities that await.

COMPLETE MENUS WITH RECIPES AND PREP TIPS

SPICED QUINOA AND CHICKPEA BOWL

PREPARATION TIME: 10 min - **COOKING TIME:** 20 min

MODE OF COOKING: Simmering - **SERVINGS:** 4

INGREDIENTS:

- 1 cup quinoa, rinsed
- 2 cups vegetable broth
- 1 can (15 oz.) chickpeas, drained and rinsed
- 1 Tbsp olive oil
- 1 tsp cumin seeds
- ½ tsp smoked paprika
- ½ tsp ground coriander
- Salt and pepper to taste
- 1 lemon, juiced
- 2 Tbsp fresh parsley, chopped

DIRECTIONS:

- In a saucepan, bring vegetable broth to a boil. Add quinoa, reduce heat, and simmer until liquid is absorbed and quinoa is fluffy.
- In a skillet, heat olive oil over medium heat. Add cumin seeds and toast until fragrant.
- Add chickpeas, smoked paprika, ground coriander, salt, and pepper. Sauté for 5 minutes.
- Combine quinoa with chickpea mixture. Stir in lemon juice and parsley before serving.

TIPS:

- Top with a dollop of Greek yogurt for creaminess.
- Garnish with toasted almonds for extra crunch.

N.V.: Calories: 280, Fat: 8g, Carbs: 42g, Protein: 10g, Sugar: 3g

HERBED ZUCCHINI NOODLES WITH WALNUT PESTO

PREPARATION TIME: 15 min - **COOKING TIME:** 5 min

MODE OF COOKING: Sautéing - **SERVINGS:** 2

INGREDIENTS:

- 2 medium zucchinis, spiralized
- 1 cup fresh basil leaves
- ¼ cup walnuts
- 1 clove garlic
- 2 Tbsp olive oil
- 2 Tbsp grated Parmesan cheese
- Salt and pepper to taste

DIRECTIONS:

- In a food processor, combine basil, walnuts, garlic, olive oil, Parmesan, salt, and pepper. Blend until smooth.
- In a skillet, heat a small amount of olive oil. Add zucchini noodles and sauté for 2-3 minutes.
- Toss noodles with walnut pesto until evenly coated. Serve immediately.

TIPS:

- Add cherry tomatoes for a burst of color and flavor.
- Use a microplane to finely grate Parmesan for a smoother pesto.

N.V.: Calories: 220, Fat: 18g, Carbs: 10g, Protein: 6g, Sugar: 4g

TURMERIC-INFUSED CAULIFLOWER STEAKS

PREPARATION TIME: 10 min - **COOKING TIME:** 30 min

MODE OF COOKING: Roasting - **SERVINGS:** 4

INGREDIENTS:

- 1 large cauliflower, cut into 1-inch thick steaks
- 2 Tbsp olive oil
- 1 tsp ground turmeric

- 1 tsp ground cumin
- Salt and pepper to taste
- 1 lime, cut into wedges

DIRECTIONS:

- Preheat oven to 400°F (204°C).
- In a small bowl, mix olive oil, turmeric, cumin, salt, and pepper.
- Brush cauliflower steaks with the spice mixture. Place on a baking sheet.
- Roast for 25-30 minutes or until golden and tender.
- Serve with lime wedges for squeezing over the steaks.

TIPS:

- Sprinkle with chopped cilantro for added freshness.
- Pair with a yogurt sauce for a cooling contrast.

N.V.: Calories: 130, Fat: 10g, Carbs: 10g, Protein: 4g, Sugar: 3g

AVOCADO AND BLACK BEAN STUFFED PEPPERS

PREPARATION TIME: 15 min - **COOKING TIME:** 25 min

MODE OF COOKING: Baking - **SERVINGS:** 4

INGREDIENTS:

- 2 large bell peppers, halved and seeded
- 1 can (15 oz.) black beans, drained and rinsed
- 1 avocado, diced
- 1 cup cooked brown rice
- 1 tsp chili powder
- 1 tsp cumin
- Salt and pepper to taste

- 1 lime, juiced
- ¼ cup fresh cilantro, chopped

DIRECTIONS:

- Preheat oven to 375°F (190°C).
- In a bowl, mix black beans, avocado, brown rice, chili powder, cumin, salt, pepper, lime juice, and cilantro.
- Stuff bell pepper halves with the mixture.
- Place stuffed peppers in a baking dish and bake for 25 minutes.

TIPS:

- Top with crumbled feta cheese for extra flavor.
- Serve with a side of salsa for added zest.

N.V.: Calories: 250, Fat: 10g, Carbs: 36g, Protein: 7g, Sugar: 4g

GINGER-SESAME SOBA NOODLES

PREPARATION TIME: 10 min - **COOKING TIME:** 10 min

MODE OF COOKING: Boiling - **SERVINGS:** 4

INGREDIENTS:

- 8 oz. soba noodles
- 2 Tbsp sesame oil
- 2 Tbsp soy sauce
- 1 Tbsp rice vinegar
- 1 Tbsp fresh ginger, grated
- 2 green onions, sliced
- 1 Tbsp sesame seeds
- 1 cup edamame, shelled

DIRECTIONS:

- Cook soba noodles according to package instructions. Drain and rinse under cold water.
- In a bowl, whisk together sesame oil, soy sauce, rice vinegar, and ginger.
- Toss noodles with sauce, green onions, sesame seeds, and edamame. Serve chilled or at room temperature.

TIPS:

- Add a drizzle of sriracha for a spicy kick.
- Garnish with nori strips for an authentic touch.

N.V.: Calories: 300, Fat: 10g, Carbs: 45g, Protein: 12g, Sugar: 2g

LEMON-DILL BAKED COD

PREPARATION TIME: 5 min - **COOKING TIME:** 20 min

MODE OF COOKING: Baking - **SERVINGS:** 4

INGREDIENTS:

- 4 cod fillets
- 2 Tbsp olive oil
- 1 lemon, sliced
- 2 Tbsp fresh dill, chopped
- Salt and pepper to taste

DIRECTIONS:

- Preheat oven to 400°F (204°C).
- Place cod fillets on a baking sheet. Drizzle with olive oil and season with salt and pepper.
- Top each fillet with lemon slices and dill.
- Bake for 15-20 minutes or until fish flakes easily with a fork.

TIPS:

- Serve with steamed asparagus for a complete meal.
- Squeeze additional lemon juice over the fish before serving for extra brightness.

N.V.: Calories: 200, Fat: 10g, Carbs: 2g, Protein: 25g, Sugar: 0g

ROASTED BEET AND ORANGE SALAD

PREPARATION TIME: 10 min - **COOKING TIME:** 40 min

MODE OF COOKING: Roasting - **SERVINGS:** 4

INGREDIENTS:

- 4 medium beets, peeled and quartered
- 2 Tbsp olive oil
- 2 oranges, segmented
- ¼ cup goat cheese, crumbled
- ¼ cup walnuts, toasted
- 2 Tbsp balsamic glaze
- Salt and pepper to taste

DIRECTIONS:

- Preheat oven to 375°F (190°C).
- Toss beets with olive oil, salt, and pepper. Roast for 35-40 minutes until tender.
- Arrange roasted beets and orange segments on a platter.
- Sprinkle with goat cheese and walnuts. Drizzle with balsamic glaze before serving.

TIPS:

- Add arugula for a peppery contrast.
- Use blood oranges for a vibrant color variation.

N.V.: Calories: 220, Fat: 14g, Carbs: 20g, Protein: 6g, Sugar: 12g

SPICY LENTIL AND TOMATO STEW

PREPARATION TIME: 10 min - **COOKING TIME:** 30 min

MODE OF COOKING: Simmering - **SERVINGS:** 4

INGREDIENTS:

- 1 cup red lentils, rinsed
- 1 Tbsp olive oil
- 1 onion, diced
- 2 cloves garlic, minced
- 1 can (14 oz.) diced tomatoes
- 1 tsp ground cumin
- ½ tsp cayenne pepper
- 4 cups vegetable broth
- Salt and pepper to taste
- 2 Tbsp fresh cilantro, chopped

DIRECTIONS:

- In a pot, heat olive oil over medium heat. Sauté onion and garlic until softened.
- Add lentils, tomatoes, cumin, cayenne, and broth. Bring to a boil.
- Reduce heat and simmer for 25-30 minutes or until lentils are tender.
- Season with salt, pepper, and cilantro before serving.

TIPS:

- Serve with crusty bread for a hearty meal.
- Adjust cayenne pepper to taste for desired spiciness.

N.V.: Calories: 250, Fat: 5g, Carbs: 40g, Protein: 12g, Sugar: 6g

TRACKING YOUR PROGRESS

Embarking on a weight loss journey with the Dr. Now 1200-Calorie Diet Plan is a transformative experience. To truly succeed, it's vital to **track your progress** effectively. Monitoring your journey not only keeps you accountable but also highlights the positive changes happening along the way.

Start by setting **realistic goals**. Consider what you want to achieve weekly and monthly. This might include weight loss targets, increased energy levels, or improved moods. Document these goals in a journal or a digital app to keep them top of mind.

Next, establish a routine for **regular check-ins**. Weigh yourself at the same time each week, under similar conditions, to maintain consistency. But remember, the scale is just one measure of success. Pay attention to how your clothes fit, your energy levels, and even your mood. These are all indicators of progress.

Consider keeping a **food diary**. Note what you eat, how much, and when. This will help you identify patterns and triggers, particularly around emotional eating. It's a powerful tool to understand your relationship with food.

Finally, celebrate your **milestones**. Whether it's losing a few pounds or resisting a tempting treat, acknowledging your achievements boosts motivation and reinforces positive behavior. Remember, every step forward is a victory in your journey to better health.

How to Use the Included Journal Effectively

Embracing the journey of weight loss can be both exciting and daunting. One of the most powerful tools at your disposal is the **journal** included in this book. It serves as your personal companion, guiding you through each step, offering insights, and helping you remain accountable. The journal is more than a log of meals and calories; it's a space for reflection and growth.

Begin by setting **clear, achievable goals**. Write them down at the start of your journal. Whether it's shedding a specific number of pounds or simply feeling more energetic, having these goals in writing makes them tangible. As you progress, revisit these goals regularly to remind yourself of your purpose.

Use the journal to **track your daily intake**, but also to note how you feel emotionally and physically. Understanding the connection between your diet and your mood can reveal patterns that may have previously gone unnoticed. This awareness is crucial in overcoming emotional eating.

Celebrate your **successes**, no matter how small. Each step forward is a victory. Document these moments to build a reservoir of motivation to draw from during challenging times. If you encounter setbacks, approach them with compassion and curiosity rather than judgment. Use your journal to explore what happened and how you can adjust your approach moving forward.

Finally, make time for **reflection**. At the end of each week, review your entries. What have you learned about yourself? What strategies have worked well, and what might need tweaking? This practice not only reinforces your commitment but also fosters a deeper understanding of your journey.

CHAPTER 9: FINAL WORDS OF ENCOURAGEMENT

As you stand on the brink of a new chapter in your life, it's important to remember that this journey is about more than just numbers on a scale. It's about reclaiming your vitality, your confidence, and your joy.

The path you've chosen is not always easy, but it is undoubtedly **worth it**. Each step forward, no matter how small, brings you closer to a healthier, more vibrant version of yourself.

Throughout this book, we've navigated the complexities of a 1200-calorie diet, tackled emotional eating, and found ways to integrate these changes into your family and social life. You've learned to view food not just as sustenance, but as a tool for healing and transformation. This isn't just a diet; it's a **lifestyle shift** that empowers you to take control of your health.

Remember, setbacks are not failures. They are opportunities to learn and grow. Be gentle with yourself, and recognize that every challenge is a chance to build resilience. Surround yourself with a supportive community, whether it's family, friends, or fellow readers who share your journey. Together, you can overcome any obstacle.

As you move forward, keep your goals in sight and your heart open to change. This is your moment to shine, to embrace the life you've always envisioned. You've got this, and we're cheering you on every step of the way.

What to Expect After 30 Days

As you wrap up the first 30 days of your journey with Dr. Now's 1200-calorie diet plan, you might be feeling a mix of excitement and curiosity about what lies ahead. The past month has been a transformative period, filled with both challenges and triumphs. Now, it's time to reflect on the **changes** you've experienced and set the stage for continued success.

Firstly, you may notice a significant improvement in your **energy levels**. By adopting a balanced diet, your body is learning to utilize nutrients more efficiently, helping you feel more vibrant and alert. This newfound energy can translate into a more active lifestyle, allowing you to engage in activities you once found daunting.

Moreover, you might find that your relationship with food has evolved. Emotional eating triggers that once seemed insurmountable are now more manageable. This is a testament to your growing ability to recognize and address the underlying emotions tied to eating habits.

As you continue, remember that the goal is not just weight loss but achieving a **sustainable lifestyle**. Celebrate your progress, no matter how small, and use it as motivation to keep moving forward. Your journey is unique, and every step you take is a step towards a healthier, more fulfilling life.

Sustaining Your Weight Loss

As you embark on this journey of **maintaining your weight loss**, remember that the key lies in consistency and adaptability. The habits you've cultivated over the past month are the foundation of your new lifestyle. However, sustaining these changes requires a commitment to ongoing **self-awareness** and **flexibility**.

First, it's crucial to **celebrate your achievements**. Recognize how far you've come, and use this as motivation to continue. This isn't just about the numbers on the scale; it's about the **increased energy**, the **confidence boost**, and the **improved well-being** you've gained. Each small victory is a step towards a healthier you.

Next, be mindful of potential triggers that could lead to setbacks. Whether it's stress, social events, or old habits creeping back, being prepared can help you stay on track. Develop strategies to cope with these challenges, such as **mindful eating** practices or seeking support from friends and family.

Remember, your diet should be **enjoyable and sustainable**. Experiment with new recipes, and don't shy away from occasional indulgences. The goal is to create a balanced lifestyle that you can maintain long-term. Keep exploring foods that nourish your body and satisfy your taste buds.

Finally, stay connected with your support network. Whether it's a community group or a trusted friend, having someone to share your journey with can provide the encouragement and accountability you need to continue thriving.

TRANSITIONING TO LONG-TERM HEALTHY HABITS

As you embark on the journey of transitioning to **long-term healthy habits**, it's essential to recognize that this is not just a diet but a **lifestyle change**. The key to success lies in embracing small, sustainable changes that gradually become part of your daily routine.

Start by **setting realistic goals**. Understand that lasting change doesn't happen overnight. Celebrate each small victory, whether it's choosing a healthier snack or completing a workout. These achievements build momentum and reinforce your commitment.

Incorporate **mindful eating** into your routine. Pay attention to your body's hunger signals and savor each bite. This practice not only enhances your relationship with food but also helps you make more conscious choices, reducing the likelihood of emotional eating.

Another crucial aspect is **planning**. Prepare your meals in advance, ensuring you have nutritious options readily available. This reduces the temptation to opt for unhealthy convenience foods when you're short on time or energy.

Remember, it's important to **stay flexible**. Life is unpredictable, and there will be times when you deviate from your plan. Rather than viewing these moments as setbacks, see them as opportunities to learn and adapt. Flexibility allows you to maintain balance and continue progressing towards your goals.

Finally, seek **support** from friends, family, or a community that understands your journey. Surrounding yourself with positive influences can provide encouragement and accountability, making the transition smoother and more enjoyable.

YOUR JOURNEY TO A HEALTHIER, HAPPIER LIFE

Embarking on a journey to better health and happiness is a courageous step, and it begins with embracing the power of **change**. Change, though often daunting, is the gateway to a life filled with renewed energy and confidence. As you take this step, remember that every small adjustment you make is a victory in itself.

Imagine waking up each day feeling more energetic, lighter, and ready to tackle whatever comes your way. This is not just a dream—it's a **realistic goal** you can achieve by following the principles outlined in this plan. The journey may have its challenges, but with each hurdle overcome, you'll gain strength and resilience.

One of the keys to success is understanding that this is a **personal journey**. What works for one person might not work for another, and that's perfectly okay. Listen to your body, learn from your experiences, and adapt the plan to fit your unique needs. Remember, you're not alone in this process; you're part of a community striving for similar goals.

As you progress, celebrate each milestone, no matter how small. These moments of triumph are what fuel your motivation and keep you moving forward. Stay committed, stay positive, and embrace the transformation that awaits you. Your healthier, happier life is within reach, and it all starts with the choices you make today.

STAYING COMMITTED TO YOUR GOALS

Embarking on a weight loss journey is much like setting sail on a vast ocean. The initial excitement fuels your motivation, but as the days go by, the waves of temptation and doubt may begin to rise. **Staying committed** to your goals requires more than just willpower; it demands a strategic approach and a compassionate mindset.

First, it's crucial to **visualize your success**. Envision the healthier, more energetic version of yourself. This mental image will serve as a guiding star, especially on days when the going gets tough. Remember, every small step you take is a stride toward that vision.

Next, consider the power of **accountability**. Share your journey with a friend or join a community of like-minded individuals. This support system will not only offer encouragement but also hold you accountable, ensuring you stay on track.

It's equally important to **celebrate your progress**. Each milestone, no matter how small, deserves recognition. Reward yourself with non-food-related treats—perhaps a new book or a relaxing spa day—to reinforce your achievements.

Finally, practice **self-compassion**. Understand that setbacks are part of the process. Instead of dwelling on them, learn and grow from each experience. By embracing your journey with kindness and patience, you'll find the strength to persevere and ultimately, reclaim your health and confidence.

APPENDICES

UNDERSTANDING NUTRITIONAL LABELS

Navigating nutritional labels can feel overwhelming, but mastering this skill is crucial for making informed dietary choices. Begin by focusing on the **serving size**, as all nutritional information is based on this measurement. Next, examine the **calories** per serving to ensure they align with your daily goals.

Pay attention to the **macronutrients**: carbohydrates, proteins, and fats. Understanding the balance of these nutrients helps you maintain a well-rounded diet. Look for **fiber** content, which aids digestion and increases satiety. Keep an eye on **sugar** levels, aiming to minimize added sugars.

Check the **sodium** content, as high sodium intake can lead to health issues like hypertension. Opt for products with lower sodium levels whenever possible. Lastly, review the **ingredients list**. Ingredients are listed in order of quantity, so be cautious of products where unhealthy components appear at the top.

MEAL PLANNING TIPS

Effective meal planning is a cornerstone of the 1200-calorie diet. Start by setting aside time each week to plan your meals. Choose **simple recipes** that fit your schedule and dietary preferences. Incorporate a variety of **fruits, vegetables, lean proteins, and whole grains** to ensure nutritional balance.

Prepare a **shopping list** based on your meal plan to avoid impulse purchases. Consider batch cooking and storing meals in portion-controlled containers to save time and reduce stress. Remember, flexibility is key—allow room for **adjustments** based on your daily needs and social commitments.

STAYING MOTIVATED

Embarking on a weight-loss journey can be challenging, but maintaining motivation is essential. Set **realistic goals** and celebrate small victories to keep your spirits high. Surround yourself with a **supportive community**—whether friends, family, or online groups—to share experiences and encouragement.

Track your progress through **journaling** or using apps to visualize your achievements. When facing setbacks, remind yourself of your initial motivations and the **positive changes** you've already made. Remember, every step forward is a step toward a healthier, more fulfilling life.

FOOD LISTS: RECOMMENDED AND AVOIDED ITEMS

Embarking on a journey to better health involves making mindful choices about the foods we consume. While the path may seem daunting, understanding which foods to embrace and which to avoid can simplify the process and empower you to make informed decisions. Remember, this is not about restriction but about nourishing your body with the right fuel.

Let's start with the **recommended foods**. These are nutrient-dense options that provide essential vitamins and minerals while helping you stay within your calorie goals. Fresh vegetables, like leafy greens, broccoli, and bell peppers, are excellent choices. They are low in calories yet high in fiber, keeping you full and satisfied. Incorporating a variety of **lean proteins** such as chicken breast, turkey, tofu, and fish can support muscle maintenance and repair, crucial for an active lifestyle. Whole grains, including quinoa, brown rice, and oats, offer sustained energy and are a great source of fiber.

Fruits, while naturally sweet, are packed with antioxidants and vitamins. Opt for berries, apples, and oranges, which provide a satisfying sweetness without excessive calories. Don't forget about healthy fats, which are essential for overall well-being. Avocados, nuts, and olive oil are fantastic options that can enhance the flavor and texture of your meals.

Now, let's address the **foods to avoid**. These are typically high in calories and low in nutritional value, making them less ideal for a 1200-calorie diet. Highly processed snacks, sugary beverages, and fried foods often contain hidden sugars and unhealthy fats that can derail your progress. It's best to steer clear of white bread, pastries, and other refined carbohydrates that offer little nutritional benefit.

Remember, this journey is about finding balance and making choices that align with your health goals. By focusing on nourishing your body with wholesome foods, you're setting the stage for a successful transformation. Stay committed, stay positive, and know that every choice you make is a step toward reclaiming your life and health.

SUBSTITUTION GUIDE: BUDGET AND TASTE-FRIENDLY OPTIONS

Embarking on a 1200-calorie diet doesn't mean sacrificing flavor or your budget. With a little creativity, you can enjoy meals that are both delicious and economical. Here's how you can make thoughtful substitutions that cater to both your palate and your wallet.

First, consider the power of **seasonal produce**. Not only are fruits and vegetables at their peak flavor when in season, but they're also more affordable. Visit your local farmers' market or grocery store to find the freshest options. For instance, swap out expensive berries in winter for apples or oranges, which are often more budget-friendly and still pack a nutritional punch.

Next, let's talk about **proteins**. Protein is crucial in keeping you full and satisfied, but it doesn't have to be pricey. Opt for plant-based proteins such as lentils, chickpeas, or beans, which are not only cost-effective but also versatile. They can be used in a variety of dishes, from hearty stews to light salads. If you prefer animal proteins, consider buying in bulk or choosing cuts like chicken thighs or ground turkey, which are typically less expensive than their leaner counterparts.

When it comes to grains, whole grains like brown rice, quinoa, and oats are not only healthy but also economical. They provide a great base for many meals and can be bought in bulk to save money. Additionally, they're filling, which is essential when you're working with a lower calorie limit.

Don't overlook the power of **herbs and spices** to transform simple ingredients into flavorful dishes. Fresh herbs can be grown at home or purchased at a low cost, and spices can be bought in small quantities to add variety to your meals without breaking the bank.

Finally, remember that cooking at home is one of the best ways to save money and control what goes into your body. Preparing meals from scratch allows you to experiment with substitutions and create dishes that satisfy both your taste buds and your budget. With these tips, you can enjoy a diverse and delicious diet while staying on track with your health goals.

FAQS: COMMON QUESTIONS ANSWERED

Embarking on the 1200-calorie diet journey can feel overwhelming, but understanding the process is key. Here are some common questions that might arise:

HOW CAN I ENSURE I'M GETTING ENOUGH NUTRIENTS?

While maintaining a **1200-calorie** intake, focus on nutrient-dense foods. Incorporate a variety of **fruits, vegetables, lean proteins,** and whole grains. These foods provide essential vitamins and minerals, ensuring your body remains nourished.

WHAT IF I FEEL HUNGRY ALL THE TIME?

It's normal to experience hunger as your body adjusts. Combat this by drinking plenty of water, eating fiber-rich foods, and ensuring your meals are balanced. Over time, your body will adapt to the new intake.

CAN I STILL ENJOY SOCIAL GATHERINGS?

Absolutely. Plan ahead by checking menus or bringing a **healthy dish** to share. Communicate your goals with friends and family, and don't hesitate to make special requests when dining out.

How do I handle setbacks?

Setbacks are part of the journey. Instead of dwelling on them, focus on your progress and recommit to your goals. Remember, **every step forward** is a victory.

Is exercise necessary on this plan?

While exercise isn't mandatory, it enhances weight loss and boosts energy. Start with activities you enjoy, gradually increasing intensity as your fitness improves.

Made in the USA
Middletown, DE
03 June 2025

76522690R00057